Professional Communication & Technical Writing Skills

NIPA® GENX ELECTRONIC RESOURCES & SOLUTIONS P. LTD.
New Delhi-110 034

About the Authors

Dr. Punam Pandey, Assistant Professor of English at **Banda University of Agriculture & Technology, UP**, has over **15 years of teaching and research experience** at undergraduate and postgraduate levels, including service at **JRD State University, Chitrakoot**. She has guided **Ph.D. and M.Phil. scholars**, authored **eight books, two manuals, two guides, and a textbook**, and published **over 50 research papers** in reputed journals. Her research interests include **British Literature, Post-Colonial Studies, and Indian Writing in English**. She, with rich experience in teaching English Literature and English Language, is equally devoted to grooming students' personalities and mentoring them towards professional excellence. A recipient of several national awards such as the **Nari Shakti Samman (2023), Rashtriya Shiksha Samman (2023), and National Education Excellence Award (2019)**, she also serves as **co-editor and board member** of national and international journals. She has frequently been invited to deliver **talks at national and international seminars/ conferences and workshops** and has also **chaired academic sessions** at various scholarly platforms.

Dr. Vipin Kumar Pandey is an **Associate Professor** at **Dr. Shakuntala Misra National Rehabilitation University, Lucknow**, with over **20 years of teaching experience**. He has authored **four books** and published **15 research papers** in journals of national and international repute. As a committed research supervisor, he has guided **Ph.D. scholars** to successful completion of their work. Dr. Pandey has played an active role in academia as a **member of Boards of Studies** and has made significant contributions to curriculum development. He has also served as the **Editor of the international journal** ***Samanubhuti***, chaired sessions at various national and international seminars and conferences, and has been recognized with **several prestigious national awards** for his academic contributions.

Professional Communication & Technical Writing Skills
A Short Guide

Punam Pandey
Assistant Professor
Banda University of Agriculture & Technology
Banda, Uttar Pradesh, India

Vipin Kumar Pandey
Associate Professor
Dr. Shakuntala Misra National Rehabilitation University
Lucknow, Uttar Pradesh, India

NIPA® GENX ELECTRONIC RESOURCES & SOLUTIONS P. LTD.
New Delhi-110 034

NIPA® GENX ELECTRONIC
RESOURCES & SOLUTIONS P. LTD.

101,103, Vikas Surya Plaza, CU Block
L.S.C.Market, Pitam Pura, New Delhi-110 034
Ph : +91 11 4386 0225, 9717133558, 9540816132
E-mail: newindiapublishingagency@gmail.com
Website: www.niparesources.com

Print ISBN: 978-93-58876-99-4

ebook ISBN: 978-93-58878-80-6

Composed and Designed by NIPA®.

Preface

Communication is the most important aspect of human life. The process of communication has become more complex and important in the current age of globalization and information technology. Communication has become an essential skill in personal, social, academic and professional life. Good communication skills increase one's ability to educate, inform, and influence others.

Today, communication skills have become essential for engineers, technologists and professionals. Industries and organizations are emphasizing the need for strong communication skills in their employees. In the modern workplace, professionals are expected to communicate effectively with colleagues, clients, managers, and stakeholders

This book, Professional Communication & Technical Writing Skills: A Short Guide, is designed to provide a comprehensive resource for learners and professionals who want to improve their communication skills in English. It covers the fundamentals of communication, the role of verbal and non-verbal communication, listening and speaking skills, and the process of writing effectively in a professional setting.

The book is structured to meet the needs of students of engineering and technology, management and business studies, and other professional courses. It offers practical guidelines, examples, and exercises to help readers enhance their communication skills.

We hope that this book will help learners develop the confidence and competence to communicate effectively in academic and professional environments.

Together, the authors bring a wealth of knowledge, research, and teaching experience, making this book a reliable and insightful guide for learners and professionals aspiring to excel in communication and technical writing

Authors

Acknowledgements

We are excited to introduce the **Professional Communication & Technical Writing Skills: A Short Guide** aims at enhancing English language proficiency for undergraduate students across all disciplines. This course features a newly developed syllabus tailored to meet students' specific needs. The accompanying guide is thoughtfully designed to help students focus on their academics more efficiently and effectively, reflecting the evolving demands of both academic and professional spheres.

It ensures students are well-prepared to excel in their studies and future careers by addressing challenges such as language barriers, technical writing skills, and cross-cultural communication. Essentially, it provides a clear path to mastering effective communication, which is vital for both professional success and personal growth.

This guide was made possible thanks to the administrative support and unwavering encouragement of **Prof. (Dr.) SVS Raju, Hon'ble Vice-Chancellor of Banda University of Agriculture & Technology, Banda,** UP whose leadership continues to inspire all university faculty.

I extend heartfelt thanks to **Prof. S.V. Dwivedi**, Dean of the College of Horticulture, for his guidance and support. I also express my sincere gratitude to **Dr. A.C. Mishra**, Director of Research at BUAT Banda, for his consistent encouragement.

A special note of thanks goes to **Dr. Vishal Chugh**, Head (In-Charge) of the Department of Basic & Social Sciences, for his guidance throughout the writing process.

We warmly welcome constructive feedback and suggestions for improvement, which will be thoughtfully incorporated into future editions.

Authors

Contents

1

Personal and Professional Communication

Objectives

- Comprehend the fundamental concepts of personal and professional communication and their significance in various contexts.
- Develop an understanding of the key elements that contribute to effective verbal and non-verbal communication.
- Identify common barriers to communication and learn strategies to overcome them in personal and professional settings.
- Enhance personal communication skills, including active listening, empathy, assertiveness, and constructive feedback.
- Acquire professional communication skills essential for writing, verbal interactions, and presentations in the workplace.
- Understand the dynamics of communication in different professional contexts, including teamwork, cross-cultural communication, and conflict resolution.

What is Communication

Communication is the process of exchanging information, thoughts, ideas, and feelings between individuals or groups. It involves the sender, message, medium, receiver, and feedback. Types of communication include personal communication, which is informal a nd characterized by emotional and personal expression, and professional communication, which is formal and involves clear messaging that follows organizational protocols.

Importance of Effective Communication: Effective communication is essential for building relationships, resolving conflicts, career advancement, and enhancing clarity and efficiency. Strong personal and professional relationships are built on clear and open communication. Good communication skills are crucial for success in the workplace, aiding in networking, team collaboration, and leadership. Clear communication reduces errors and improves overall efficiency.

Elements of Communication: Verbal communication involves the use of spoken or written words to convey messages, including tone of vo ice, vocabulary, clarity, and brevity. Non- verbal communication encompasses body language, facial expressions, gestures, posture, and eye contact, often conveying more meaning than words. Key aspects of non-verbal communication include facial expressions that convey emotions, gestures that emphasize points, posture reflecting confidence, and eye contact that builds trust.

Barriers to Communication: Understanding barriers to communication can help improve interactions. Common barriers include physical barriers such as noise or distance, psychological barriers stemming from emotional states or biases, language barriers due to differences in language or jargon, and cultural barriers arising from variations in cultural norms. Strategies to overcome barriers include actively listening, using simple language, being aware of non-verbal cues, and fostering an inclusive environment.

Personal Communication Skills: Effective personal communication skills include active listening, empathy, assertiveness, and providing feedback. Active listening engages with the speaker to understand their message and respond thoughtfully. Empathy involves understanding and sharing the feelings of others. Assertiveness allows individuals to express thoughts openly while respecting others, and feedback should be constructive and open to reception.

Professional Communication Skills: Effective communication skills are critical in professional settings for written communication, such as emails that require clear subject lines and concise content, and reports that should be well-organized and factual. Verbal communication in professional settings includes conducting meetings with prepared agendas and taking minutes, participating in interviews by answering questions confidently, and networking to build connections through effective conversation.

Communication in Different Professional Contexts: Team communication fosters collaboration and productivity through regular check-ins and open forums for sharing ideas. In cross-cultural communication, awareness of cultural differences is vital, requiring respect for cultural norms and adaptability in communication styles. For conflict resolution, effective communication involves remaining calm, focusing on the issue, and finding solutions collaboratively.

Questions

1. Explain the concept of communication and its significance in both personal and professional contexts.
2. Discuss the various types of communication and provide examples of each.
3. Analyze the role of non-verbal communication in conveying messages.
4. Identify and explain common barriers to effective communication.
5. Evaluate the importance of active listening in personal and professional communication.
6. Describe how assertiveness differs from aggression in communication.
7. Examine the impact of cultural differences on communication styles.
8. Discuss the significance of feedback in the communication process.
9. Analyze the communication skills necessary for effective teamwork.
10. Reflect on the role of technology in personal and professional communication.

2

Importance of Language and Communication Skills in the Engineering Profession

Objectives

- To understand the critical role of language and communication skills in engineering.
- To explore how communication impacts the effectiveness and efficiency of engineering work.
- To examine the types of communication skills necessary for engineers
- To highlight the significance of these skills in teamwork, leadership, and project management.
- To discuss the challenges engineers face in communication and how to overcome them.
- To encourage students to develop and enhance their communication skills for better academic and professional outcomes.

Introduction

Language and communication skills are integral to the engineering profession, often determining the success or failure of projects. Engineers are required not only to excel in their technical expertise but also to effectively convey their ideas, collaborate with diverse teams, and manage complex projects. This necessitates a high level of proficiency in both language and communication skills.

The Role of Communication in Engineering

Effective communication serves as the backbone of the engineering profession. It is essential in every phase of an engineer's work, from conceptualization to implementation. Communication bridges the gap between technical knowledge and practical application, ensuring that ideas are shared accurately and effectively.

1. **Knowledge Sharing:** Engineers must communicate complex information to clients, stakeholders, and team members. Clear communication prevents misunderstandings and ensures that everyone is on the same page.
2. **Decision Making:** Effective communication aids in making informed decisions. Engineers must explain their analysis and reasoning to guide stakeholders towards the best solutions.
3. **Safety and Compliance:** Miscommunication in safety protocols, design specifications, or regulatory compliance can lead to significant risks. Clear communication minimizes these risks.

Types of Communication Skills Essential for Engineers

Understanding the various types of communication skills is crucial for engineers. These skills help in different contexts, whether working with a team or presenting to clients.

Verbal Communication

- Used in meetings, presentations, and daily interactions.
- Requires clarity, confidence, and the ability to explain complex concepts in simple terms.
- Enhances interpersonal skills and helps in building rapport with colleagues and clients.

Written Communication

- Involves writing reports, emails, proposals, and technical documentation.
- Requires precision, conciseness, and attention to detail.
- Essential for documenting processes, creating manuals, and ensuring that information is accessible and understandable.

Non-verbal Communication

- Includes body language, eye contact, facial expressions, and gestures.
- Conveys confidence, openness, and empathy, enhancing the effectiveness of verbal communication.
- Important in interviews, presentations, and negotiations where first impressions matter.

Listening Skills

- Active listening ensures understanding of instructions, feedback, and concerns.

- Involves asking clarifying questions and providing feedback to confirm understanding.
- Critical in collaborative settings to ensure smooth workflow and problem-solving.

Importance of Communication in Teamwork and Leadership

Communication skills are fundamental to effective teamwork and leadership in engineering.

Teamwork

- Collaboration requires sharing ideas, debating solutions, and working together towards a common goal.
- Engineers often work in interdisciplinary teams, requiring them to communicate with professionals from other fields.
- Effective communication reduces conflicts and enhances team productivity.

Leadership

- Leaders must motivate, guide, and influence their teams. Communication is key to inspiring confidence and directing efforts.
- Clear communication helps in delegating tasks, providing constructive feedback, and resolving conflicts.

Project Management

- Involves planning, executing, and monitoring projects. Engineers must communicate with various stakeholders to ensure the project stays on track.
- Effective communication helps in managing resources, time, and expectations.

Enhancing Communication Skills in Engineering

To excel in communication, engineers must actively work on improving their skills through continuous learning and practice.

Language Proficiency

- Proficiency in English, the global language of engineering, is often essential. Engineers should also be open to learning other relevant languages based on their work environment.

- Technical vocabulary and industry-specific jargon should be mastered, along with the ability to simplify this language for broader audiences.

Soft Skills Training

- Participating in workshops, courses, or training programs on public speaking, technical writing, and interpersonal communication can significantly enhance skills.
- Practicing presentation skills with peers or mentors helps in gaining confidence and improving delivery.

Use of Technology

- Familiarity with communication tools like video conferencing software, collaborative platforms (e.g., Slack, Microsoft Teams), and presentation software (e.g., PowerPoint) is essential.
- Digital literacy aids in conveying information efficiently, especially in remote or global work environments.

Feedback Mechanisms

- Regular feedback from supervisors, colleagues, and clients helps in identifying areas for improvement.
- Engineers should be open to constructive criticism and use it to refine their communication strategies.

Challenges in Communication for Engineers

Despite its importance, communication can be challenging for engineers, particularly when it involves conveying technical information to non-technical audiences.

Technical Jargon

- Overuse of jargon can lead to confusion among stakeholders who do not have a technical background. Engineers need to adjust their language based on the audience.

Cultural and Linguistic Barriers

- In global teams, cultural differences can impact communication styles. Understanding and respecting these differences is crucial for effective collaboration.

- Language barriers may arise when working with international teams, requiring patience and adaptability.

Digital Communication Challenges

- With increased reliance on digital communication, misinterpretations can occur due to the lack of face-to-face interaction. Clarity in written communication is essential to overcome this barrier.

Impact of Poor Communication Skills in Engineering

The consequences of inadequate communication skills in engineering can be severe, affecting project outcomes, team dynamics, and individual careers.

Project Failures

- Miscommunication can lead to errors, project delays, and increased costs. For example, unclear instructions may result in the wrong specifications being followed.

Client Dissatisfaction

- Inability to communicate effectively with clients can result in unmet expectations and loss of business.

Career Limitations

- Engineers with poor communication skills may struggle to move into leadership roles or may be overlooked for promotions.

Strategies to Improve Communication Skills

To address these challenges, engineers can adopt various strategies to improve their communication skills.

Public Speaking and Presentation Skills

- Joining groups like Toastmasters can help build confidence in public speaking.

  Practice delivering technical presentations to different audiences.

Writing Practice

- Engage in writing activities, such as blogging, to refine written communication skills. Regularly review and edit your work for clarity and conciseness.

Interactive Learning

- Participate in team activities, simulations, or role-playing exercises to enhance communication in real-world scenarios.

Language and communication skills are not just supplementary to technical expertise in engineering; they are critical components that significantly impact an engineer's effectiveness and career trajectory. By investing in developing these skills, engineers can enhance their professional success, contribute more effectively to their teams, and navigate the complex challenges of the engineering profession.

Questions

1. What are the key roles of communication skills in the engineering profession? Provide examples from real-world scenarios.
2. Explain the significance of verbal and non-verbal communication skills for engineers. How do these skills complement each other?
3. Identify common communication challenges faced by engineers and suggest ways to overcome them with examples.
4. How can poor communication impact project outcomes in engineering? Discuss with case studies or hypothetical situations.
5. What strategies can engineers use to improve their communication skills? Provide practical suggestions for implementation.
6. Discuss the role of communication skills in teamwork and leadership within engineering. Why are these skills critical for engineers aspiring to be team leaders?
7. How can engineers balance technical language with the need to communicate effectively with non-technical stakeholders? Provide tips and examples.
8. Why is feedback important in the process of improving communication skills?
9. Discuss methods engineers can use to seek and apply feedback.

3

Communication and Its Models

Objectives

- To understand the meaning and importance of communication.
- To explore the basic components and process of communication.
- To identify the different types and forms of communication.
- To recognize barriers to effective communication and strategies to overcome them.
- To develop an appreciation for the role of communication in personal and professional contexts.

Meaning and Importance of Communication

Communication is the process of exchanging information, ideas, emotions, and messages between individuals or groups. It is a fundamental aspect of human interaction and plays a vital role in personal, social, and professional contexts. Effective communication enables understanding, fosters relationships, and facilitates decision-making.

Key Importance

- **Personal Growth:** Enhances self-expression and emotional intelligence.
- **Professional Success:** Essential for teamwork, leadership, and conflict resolution.
- **Social Connectivity:** Strengthens relationships and community bonds.

Components and Process of Communication

Communication involves several core components and follows a systematic process.

Components

1. **Sender:** The individual or entity initiating the message.
2. **Message:** The content or information being conveyed.

3. **Medium:** The channel used to deliver the message (e.g., verbal, written).
4. **Receiver:** The person or audience receiving the message.
5. **Feedback:** The response from the receiver, confirming understanding.

Process

1. **Idea Generation:** Formulating the content of the message.
2. **Encoding:** Translating ideas into words, symbols, or gestures.
3. **Transmission:** Sending the message through a chosen medium.
4. **Decoding:** Interpreting the message by the receiver.
5. **Feedback:** Ensuring the message was understood as intended.

Types and Forms of Communication

Types of Communication

1. **Verbal Communication:** Exchange of information through spoken or written words.
2. **Non-Verbal Communication:** Use of gestures, facial expressions, body language, and tone of voice.
3. **Visual Communication:** Conveying messages through images, charts, and graphs.

Forms of Communication

1. **Intrapersonal Communication:** Communication within oneself, such as self- reflection.
2. **Interpersonal Communication:** Direct interaction between individuals or small groups.
3. **Group Communication:** Interaction within a collective or organizational setting.
4. **Mass Communication:** Dissemination of messages to large audiences via media.

Communication is the cornerstone of human interaction, influencing every aspect of life. Understanding its basics—from types and processes to barriers and applications—is essential for personal and professional growth. By mastering communication skills, individuals can express themselves effectively, build strong relationships, and achieve success in their endeavors.

Popular Communication Models

1. Shannon-Weaver Model (1949)

Key Components: Sender, Encoder, Channel, Decoder, Receiver, Noise, Feedback.

Description: Known as the "mother of all models," this linear model explains communication as a one-way process initially. The sender encodes a message, transmits it through a channel, and the receiver decodes it. Feedback was later introduced, making it a two-way process. Noise represents any interference that affects the clarity of the message.

2. Berlo's SMCR Model (1960)

Key Components: Source, Message, Channel, Receiver.

Description: This model highlights the importance of four elements:

Source: The sender's communication skills, attitude, knowledge, and social system.

Message: Content, structure, and elements of the message.

Channel: Medium through which the message is transmitted (e.g., hearing, seeing).

Receiver: The recipient's skills, attitude, and knowledge.

2. Interactive Model

Key Components: Sender, Receiver, Feedback, Noise.

Description: Highlights the two-way nature of communication where roles alternate between sender and receiver. Feedback plays a critical role in ensuring the message is understood as intended. Noise can distort the feedback or the original message.

3. Transactional Model

Key Components: Communicators, Messages, Context, Feedback, Noise.

Description: This model views communication as a dynamic process where communicators simultaneously send and receive messages. It acknowledges the relational and situational context, making it ideal for real-time conversations.

(logical argument).

4. Westley and MacLean's Model (1957)

Key Components: Context, Communicators, Feedback.

Description: Explains mass communication processes and highlights the role of contextual factors. The model accounts for environmental influences and how messages are created, disseminated, and interpreted.

Understanding these models helps professionals, educators, and students to grasp the nuances of communication processes, enabling them to enhance their skills in various contexts. Each model has unique applications and is relevant depending on the communication scenario.

Questions

1. Define communication and explain its importance in daily life.
2. List and describe the basic components of the communication process.
3. Differentiate between verbal and non-verbal communication with examples.
4. Identify common barriers to effective communication and suggest strategies to overcome them.
5. Discuss the role of communication in a professional context.
6. What are the key components of the communication process?
7. Define communication and explain its importance in professional and personal contexts.
8. What are the differences between verbal and non-verbal communication?
9. Describe Shannon and Weaver's model of communication and its significance.
10. Explain the role of feedback in the communication process.
11. Compare and contrast linear and interactive communication models.
12. How can one improve their listening skills for better communication?
13. What are the advantages and disadvantages of using technology in communication?
14. How can one effectively manage communication in a multicultural environment?
15. Explain Berlo's SMCR model of communication.
16. How does communication evolve with advancements in technology?
17. Discuss the importance of audience analysis in preparing communication materials.

4

Communication Process Meaning, Types, and Models

Objectives

- Understand the meaning of the communication process.
- Learn the various types of communication.
- Explore different models of communication.
- Analyze how communication flows in different contexts.

Meaning of Communication Process

The **communication process** refers to the systematic steps through which a message is conveyed from a sender to a receiver. It involves the transmission of information through a medium, with feedback confirming whether the message has been received and understood correctly.

Elements of the Communication Process

The communication process consists of the following elements:

- **Sender:** The person or entity initiating the message.
- **Message:** The content or information to be communicated.
- **Encoding:** The process of converting the message into symbols, language, or signals that can be understood by the receiver.
- **Medium/Channel:** The pathway through which the message is transmitted (e.g., face-to-face, email, phone).
- **Receiver:** The person or entity for whom the message is intended.
- **Decoding:** The process by which the receiver interprets and understands the message.
- **Feedback:** The response of the receiver that indicates whether the message was understood.

Types of Communication

Communication can be classified into different types based on the context and method of delivery:

a) Verbal Communication

- Involves the use of spoken or written words to convey a message.
- Examples: Conversations, speeches, letters, emails.

b) Non-verbal Communication

- Involves the transmission of messages through body language, facial expressions, gestures, and posture.
- Examples: Eye contact, facial expressions, body movements.

c) Visual Communication

- The use of visual elements like images, charts, diagrams, or videos to communicate.
- Examples: Graphs, infographics, slideshows.

d) Formal and Informal Communication

- **Formal communication** follows official channels within an organization (e.g., reports, memos).
- **Informal communication** takes place casually between individuals (e.g., casual chats).

Improving the Communication Process

Effective communication requires attention to several factors:

- **Clarity of Message:** Ensure the message is concise and to the point.
- **Medium Selection:** Choose the most appropriate channel based on the audience and message.
- **Feedback Loops:** Encourage receivers to provide feedback, ensuring the message is understood.
- **Active Engagement:** Both senders and receivers should be actively involved in the communication process, ensuring understanding.

The communication process is a complex and dynamic interaction involving multiple elements. Understanding the types of communication and applying different models can enhance the effectiveness of message transmission in various contexts, from personal conversations to organizational communication.

Questions

1. Define the term 'Communication Process'. Explain its essential elements with suitable examples.
2. Describe the different types of communication with examples. How are verbal and non-verbal communications different from each other?
3. What are the major models of communication? Briefly explain any two models with the help of diagrams.
4. Discuss the importance of understanding the communication process in academic and professional settings.
5. How does feedback play a vital role in the communication process? Illustrate with real-life examples.
6. Differentiate between linear, interactive, and transactional models of communication. Which model do you think is most effective and why?

5

Communication Gap and Its Reasons

Objectives

- Understand the concept of communication gap.
- Identify the reasons behind communication gaps in personal, professional, and organizational settings.
- Explore the effects of communication gaps on relationships and productivity.
- Develop strategies to overcome communication gaps effectively.

Communication Gap

A communication gap occurs when there is a breakdown in the communication process, leading to misunderstandings, incomplete information transfer, or misinterpretation of messages. It can happen between individuals, groups, or organizations, and has significant impacts on relationships, productivity, and decision-making.

Reasons for Communication Gaps

Several factors contribute to communication gaps. These reasons can be categorized into three broad areas: individual, organizational, and technological.

a) Individual Factors

- **Cultural Differences:** People from different cultures may interpret words and body language differently, leading to miscommunication.
- **Perception Differences:** Each person filters information through their own experiences and biases, which can lead to communication breakdowns.
- **Language Barriers:** Language differences or poor command of the communication language can prevent clear message delivery.
- **Emotional Barriers:** Stress, anxiety, or emotional states can distort how a message is sent and received.

- **Assumptions:** Assuming the receiver already knows certain information can result in incomplete communication.

b) Organizational Factors

- **Hierarchy and Power Structures:** Information may not flow freely in hierarchical organizations, leading to gaps in understanding.
- **ack of Feedback:** Without feedback, senders are unaware if their message was correctly understood, creating a gap.
- **Overload of Information:** Too much information can overwhelm the receiver, causing them to miss critical details.
- **Physical Barriers:** Poor office layouts, lack of access to technology, or remote work situations can obstruct clear communication.

c) Technological Factors:

- **Misuse of Communication Tools:** Over-reliance on email, texts, or instant messaging without face-to-face communication can lead to misinterpretation.
- **Incompatibility of Technology:** Different platforms and tools not being integrated properly can lead to communication gaps.
- **Delayed Responses:** In asynchronous communication, delays between sending and receiving messages can cause confusion.

Effects of Communication Gaps

Communication gaps can lead to various negative outcomes

- **Decreased Productivity:** In the workplace, communication gaps can result in project delays, mistakes, or inefficiencies.
- **Conflicts and Misunderstandings:** Personal relationships may suffer due to unaddressed or misunderstood concerns.
- **Reduced Employee Morale:** In an organizational context, communication gaps can create frustration and disengagement among employees.
- **Poor Decision-Making:** Incomplete information leads to incorrect conclusions, hampering decision-making processes.

Strategies to Overcome Communication Gaps

To overcome communication gaps, the following strategies can be employed:

- **Active Listening:** Pay close attention to the speaker and ask clarifying questions.

- **Feedback Mechanisms:** Encourage two-way communication and verify the message was understood as intended.
- **Cultural Sensitivity:** Be aware of cultural differences and adapt communication styles accordingly.
- **Training Programs:** Conduct communication skill workshops in organizations to equip employees with the necessary tools.
- **Utilization of Technology:** Use integrated communication platforms that ensure smooth flow and easy tracking of conversations.

"He who asks is a fool for five minutes, but he who does not ask remains a fool forever."

This proverb emphasizes the importance of asking questions and seeking clarification in communication to avoid misunderstandings or gaps. A **communication gap** often arises when people fail to ask for clarification or hesitate to express their thoughts, leaving room for ambiguity and misinterpretation. The proverb encourages overcoming the fear of appearing uninformed and stresses the value of open communication. It highlights that by addressing questions or concerns, one can prevent the gap in understanding from widening, thus fostering clearer and more effective communication.

Understanding the causes of communication gaps is crucial for improving relationships and efficiency in personal and organizational environments. By addressing the underlying issues and implementing clear communication strategies, one can minimize misunderstandings and enhance overall communication effectiveness.

Questions

1. Define a communication gap and explain its significance in personal and organizational contexts.
2. Discuss the individual factors that contribute to communication gaps. Provide examples to illustrate your points.
3. Explain how organizational factors like hierarchy and lack of feedback can create communication gaps. Suggest ways to mitigate these issues.
4. Analyze the role of technology in causing communication gaps. What measures can be taken to minimize these gaps?
5. Describe the effects of communication gaps on workplace productivity and employee morale.
6. What is the importance of active listening in overcoming communication gaps? Provide practical examples of how it can be implemented effectively.

7. How do cultural differences and language barriers lead to communication gaps?

   Suggest strategies to address these challenges in a multicultural environment.
8. Reflect on the proverb, "He who asks is a fool for five minutes, but he who does not ask remains a fool forever," in the context of communication gaps. Discuss its relevance with examples.
9. List and elaborate on the strategies that can be used to overcome communication gaps in an organization.
10. Why is understanding the causes of communication gaps essential for enhancing overall communication effectiveness? Discuss with examples from real-life situations.

6

Non-Linguistic Barriers to Communication

Objectives

- Understand what non-linguistic barriers to communication are and how they affect the communication process.
- Identify different types of non-linguistic barriers and provide examples of each.
- Recognize the impact of non-linguistic barriers on personal and professional communication.
- Learn strategies to overcome non-linguistic barriers to enhance effective communication.
- Develop skills to create a more inclusive and understanding communication environment.

Introduction to Non-Linguistic Barriers

Non-linguistic barriers to communication refer to obstacles that hinder the effective exchange of information and ideas but do not stem from language itself. These barriers can arise from a variety of sources, including emotional, physical, social, and environmental factors. Unlike linguistic barriers, which involve issues related to language, vocabulary, or grammar, non- linguistic barriers affect how messages are received and interpreted.

Understanding these barriers is crucial for improving communication skills, as they can significantly impact personal relationships, workplace dynamics, and social interactions. Effective communication goes beyond just the words spoken; it also involves understanding the context in whch communication occurs.

Types of Non-Linguistic Barriers

Non-linguistic barriers can be categorized into several types, each with its own characteristics and implications:

Physical Barriers

Physical barriers are environmental factors that obstruct communication. These include noise, distance, and inadequate technology. For example, loud background noise in a restaurant can hinder a conversation, making it difficult for participants to hear each other clearly. Similarly, in a workplace setting, an open-office layout can contribute to distractions that make focused conversations challenging. Physical barriers can also arise from technological limitations, such as poor internet connectivity during virtual meetings.

Emotional Barriers

Emotional states can cloud judgment and affect how individuals communicate and perceive messages. For instance, if someone is upset or angry, they may misinterpret neutral comments as negative or critical, leading to unnecessary conflict. Stress and anxiety can also hinder one's ability to listen actively or articulate thoughts clearly. Recognizing and managing these emotional barriers is essential for maintaining effective communication.

Cultural Barriers

Cultural differences can lead to misunderstandings in communication styles, norms, and expectations. For example, gestures or body language that are acceptable in one culture may be considered offensive in another. Additionally, varying communication styles—such as direct versus indirect communication—can create confusion. It's essential to be culturally aware and sensitive to different communication practices, especially in diverse environments.

Social Barriers

Social barriers arise from social hierarchies, power dynamics, and group relationships. For example, a subordinate may feel hesitant to express their opinion in a meeting dominated by senior management due to perceived power dynamics. This can lead to a lack of diverse perspectives and hinder creativity and problem-solving within a team. Recognizing social structures and creating an inclusive environment can mitigate these barriers.

Perceptual Barriers

Differences in perception and interpretation of messages can lead to miscommunication. Each individual's background, experiences, and beliefs shape how they interpret information. For instance, two people may interpret the same situation differently based on their unique perspectives, leading to confusion and misunderstandings. It is vital to clarify assumptions and seek common ground to overcome perceptual barriers.

Impact of Non-Linguistic Barriers

Non-linguistic barriers can significantly impact both personal and professional communication. In personal relationships, these barriers can lead to misunderstandings, misinterpretations, and unresolved conflicts. For example, emotional barriers may prevent open discussions, resulting in built-up resentment.

In professional settings, non-linguistic barriers can hinder teamwork, collaboration, and productivity. For instance, if employees feel uncomfortable due to social barriers, they may refrain from sharing valuable ideas, thus stifling innovation and growth. In team meetings, if members are not encouraged to speak up due to cultural or social barriers, the overall effectiveness of the team can be compromised.

Recognizing and addressing these barriers is crucial for fostering an environment that promotes effective communication and collaboration.

Strategies to Overcome Non-Linguistic Barriers

To enhance communication and minimize the impact of non-linguistic barriers, individuals and organizations can implement several strategies:

Enhance Awareness

Recognizing the presence of non-linguistic barriers is the first step in overcoming them. Being aware of emotional states, cultural differences, and environmental factors can help individuals adjust their communication strategies. Self-awareness and empathy are crucial for identifying and addressing these barriers in oneself and others.

Active Listening

Practicing active listening can improve understanding and reduce misinterpretation. This involves fully concentrating on the speaker, acknowledging their message, and responding thoughtfully. Techniques such as paraphrasing and asking clarifying questions can further enhance active listening skills.

Adapt Communication Styles

Tailoring communication styles to fit the audience's cultural background and emotional state can foster better understanding. For instance, using simpler language when speaking to someone who may be feeling overwhelmed can help convey the message more clearly. Understanding the preferred communication styles of different cultures can also aid in reducing misunderstandings.

Create a Conducive Environment

Minimizing physical distractions and ensuring a comfortable setting for conversations can enhance communication. For example, finding a quiet place to discuss important matters can facilitate clearer exchanges. In professional settings, creating designated quiet zones or using technology to reduce background noise can improve focus and engagement.

Encourage Openness

Fostering an open communication culture encourages individuals to express their thoughts and feelings without fear of judgment. This can be achieved through regular check-ins and creating safe spaces for dialogue. Encouraging feedback and showing appreciation for diverse opinions can promote a more inclusive environment.

Non-linguistic barriers to communication can significantly hinder effective exchanges of information and ideas. By understanding these barriers and implementing strategies to overcome them, individuals can improve their communication skills, leading to more effective interactions in both personal and professional settings. This study material aims to equip students with the knowledge and tools to navigate non-linguistic barriers, enhancing their overall communication effectiveness.

Through increased awareness and active efforts to address non-linguistic barriers, individuals can foster more meaningful connections and build healthier relationships, both personally and professionally.

Questions

1. Define non-linguistic barriers to communication and explain their significance in the communication process.
2. Identify and describe at least four different types of non-linguistic barriers. Provide examples for each type.
3. Discuss the impact of emotional barriers on effective communication. How can these barriers affect interpersonal relationships?
4. Explain how cultural barriers can lead to misunderstandings in communication. What strategies can be used to overcome these barriers?

5. Analyze the role of physical barriers in communication. What are some common physical barriers that individuals might encounter in different settings?
6. What are perceptual barriers, and how do they influence the interpretation of messages? Provide an example to illustrate your point.
7. Discuss the importance of active listening in overcoming non-linguistic barriers. What techniques can enhance active listening skills?
8. Describe the impact of social barriers on workplace communication. How can organizations create an inclusive environment that minimizes these barriers?
9. How can self-awareness and empathy contribute to addressing non-linguistic barriers in communication?
10. Reflect on a personal experience where a non-linguistic barrier affected your communication. What strategies did you use to overcome it, or what could have been done differently?

7

Writing Process and Its Stages

Objectives

- Understand the stages of the writing process.
- Visualize the flow of writing stages using a graph.
- Apply effective strategies for each stage of writing.

Introduction

The writing process is a structured approach that helps writers create clear and coherent texts. It generally consists of five main stages: prewriting, drafting, revising, editing, and publishing. The stages are interconnected, and writers often cycle back to earlier steps before finalizing their work. The following graph will help visualize how these stages overlap and repeat during the writing process.

Graph of the Writing Process

The graph below represents the cyclical nature of the writing process:

Prewriting

↓

Drafting

↗↘

Revising Editing

↓

Publishing

This graph shows that while each stage is distinct, writers often move back and forth between **Drafting**, **Revising**, and **Editing** before reaching the **Publishing** stage. Prewriting sets the foundation, and once the first draft is created, it may be revised and edited several times.

1. Prewriting

Definition: Prewriting is the planning phase where the writer generates ideas, researches, and organizes thoughts before starting the draft.

Key Activities

- **Brainstorming:** Think of all potential ideas related to the topic.
- **Mind Mapping:** Create a visual representation of ideas and how they connect.
- **Outlining:** Organize the key points and structure of the text.
- **Researching:** Gather relevant information and resources for the topic.

2. Drafting

Definition: Drafting is the stage where the writer begins to turn ideas into sentences and paragraphs, forming a rough version of the text.

Key Tips

- **Get ideas on paper:** Focus on getting thoughts down without worrying about perfection.
- **Follow the outline:** Use the prewriting plan as a guide to keep writing focused.
- **Leave room for improvement:** Don't aim for the final version in this stage.

3. Revising

Definition: In the revising stage, the writer reviews and improves the content by focusing on clarity, organization, and coherence.

Key Areas to Address

- **Structure:** Ensure the content flows logically from one point to another.
- **Content:** Add, remove, or rearrange ideas to make the text more effective.
- **Clarity:** Reword unclear sections to improve understanding.

Revising Process Graphically

Prewriting → Drafting ↔ Revising → Editing → Publishing

Revising often involves moving back to **Drafting** as the writer refines ideas.

4. Editing

Definition: Editing involves correcting errors in grammar, punctuation, spelling, and ensuring consistency in style.

Key Tasks

- **Grammar and Syntax:** Check for subject-verb agreement, sentence structure, and tense consistency.
- **Punctuation:** Ensure proper use of commas, periods, semicolons, etc.
- **Spelling:** Correct any spelling mistakes or typos.
- **Formatting:** Ensure the text meets style guide requirements (e.g., APA, MLA).

Editing Process Graphically

Copy code

Drafting ↔ Revising ↔ Editing → Publishing

Editing may overlap with revising, but it focuses more on technical corrections.

5. Publishing

Definition: Publishing is the stage where the final draft is shared with an audience, whether in print or digitally.

Key Considerations

- **Audience:** Tailor the text to suit the intended readers.
- **Presentation:** Format the work appropriately for print, online, or verbal presentation.
- **Feedback:** Be open to further revisions after feedback from the audience.

Graphical Summary of the Writing Process

Prewriting
↓
Drafting
↕
Revising
↓
Editing
↓
Publishing

This graph highlights that feedback can come after revising, editing, or even after publishing, as writers continuously seek to improve their work.

The writing process is flexible, and the stages are not strictly linear. Writers may revisit earlier stages multiple times. By following a structured approach and using feedback loops, the final product will be clear, engaging, and well-organized.

Questions

1. What is the main purpose of the prewriting stage?
2. Describe the difference between revising and editing.
3. How can feedback be integrated into the writing process?
4. Why is the drafting stage important even if it's not the final version?
5. How does publishing differ from the other stages of the writing process?

8

The Art of Note-Taking

Objectives

- Assists in retaining and recalling key information.
- Enhances focus and concentration during learning activities.
- Serves as a personalized summary of complex content.
- Provides an invaluable resource for exam preparation and academic success.

Note-Taking

Note-taking is the process of systematically recording important information from lectures, readings, or discussions to enhance understanding, memory retention, and future reference. It is a fundamental academic skill that not only aids comprehension but also fosters active engagement with the material.

Methods of Note-Taking

To cater to diverse learning preferences, several note-taking methods have been developed. Understanding these techniques enables learners to adopt the most effective strategy for their needs.

a. The Cornell Method

The Cornell Method provides an efficient and structured way to organize and summarize notes without the need for extensive rewriting. Start by recording notes in the main section and use the left-hand margin to highlight key ideas, keywords, or cues.

Steps to Follow

- Divide your page by drawing a 2-inch margin on the left, leaving a 6-inch section on the right for note-taking.
- During the lecture, jot down information in the larger area.
- When the instructor transitions to a new topic, leave a few blank lines before continuing.

- After the class, refine your notes by completing phrases and sentences for clarity.
- In the left margin, write cues or keywords for each key point.

Structure

- **Notes Section:** Used to jot down main ideas, facts, and supporting details during the lecture.
- **Cues Section:** Reserved for keywords, questions, or prompts that aid memory and comprehension.
- **Summary Section:** A concise overview of the content in your own words, written after class.

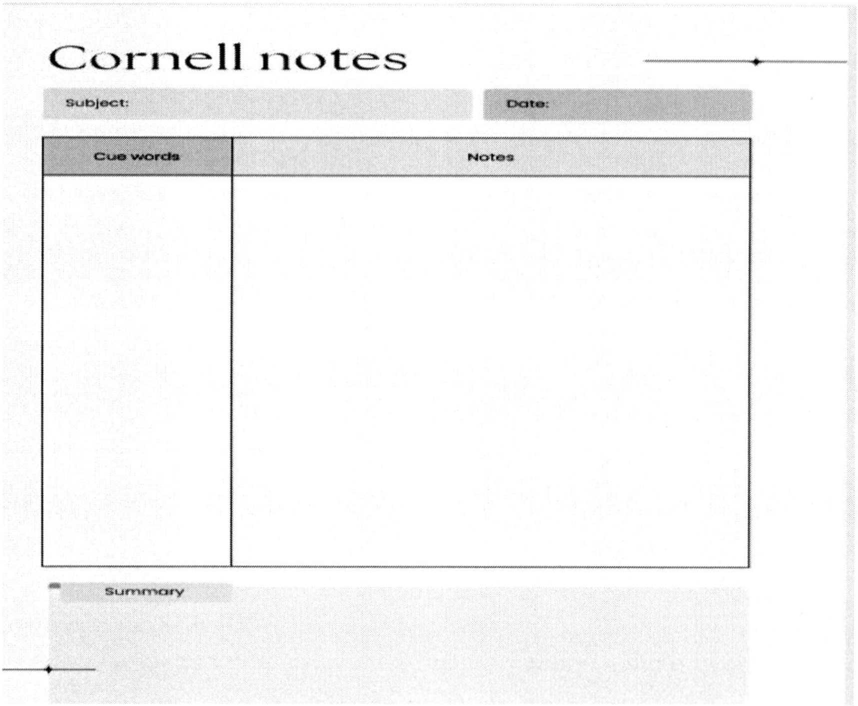

Image: Cornell's note taking Template

Advantages of the Cornell Method

- Ensures notes are well-organized and systematic for both recording and review.
- Facilitates easy identification of main concepts and ideas.
- Simple, effective, and time-saving.

Best Use

Ideal for note-taking in any lecture setting.

b. The Outline Method

Description: This method organizes information hierarchically using main headings and subheadings, making it ideal for subjects with a logical structure.

Advantages

Facilitates a clear and logical arrangement of topics.

Disadvantages

- Less effective for lectures with a rapid pace or unstructured delivery.

c. Mind Mapping

Description: A visual technique that represents information through diagrams, connecting concepts and ideas in a web-like structure.

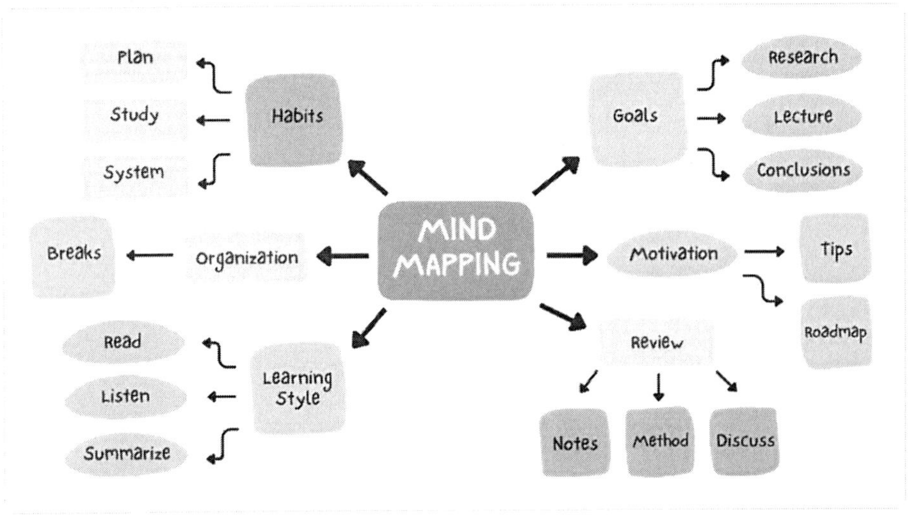

Benefits

- Ideal for brainstorming sessions and visual learners.
- Encourages creative thinking and the exploration of relationships between topics.

How to Use

- Start with a central topic at the center of the page.
- Branch out into related subtopics and details, connecting them visually.

d. The Charting Method

Description: This technique involves dividing the page into columns, each labeled with a category, to organize detailed information.

Anxiety Disorder.	**Details**	**Duration/Frequency**
Generalized Anxiety Disorder	Always Tense; Continually Aroused Autoj/ Ortlc ^Egvous System *(High Blood* Pressure *Adt> Heav* Kate, Fluscle Ache)	Fear Lasts Longer Than 6 Aonths
Social Phobia	Extreme Self-Consciousness, Concern of Offendfng Others, Avoidance of Social Interactions	Fear Lasts Longer Than 6 Months
Agoraphobia	Avoidance of Rlrces or Situations that Aav Trigger Panic	Fear Lasts Longer Than 6 Aonths

Best for

- Subjects involving comparisons, statistics, or chronological events, such as history or science.

How to Use

- Label columns with specific headings.
- Fill in relevant details under each category during the lecture.

Advantages

- Simplifies complex information into a structured table.
- Allows for easy comparison and contrast.

3. Tips for Effective Note-Taking

To maximize the benefits of note-taking, consider the following strategies:

a) Preparation

- Review previous material to build context.
- Bring essential tools, whether traditional (notebooks, pens) or digital (laptops, tablets).

b) Active Listening

Focus on understanding key concepts instead of transcribing everything verbatim.

c) Abbreviations and Symbols

Develop a shorthand system to save time and increase efficiency.

d) Post-Class Review

Edit and clarify notes promptly to ensure accuracy and comprehension.

e) Systematic Organization

Group notes by topic or subject for easier retrieval.

4. Using Digital Tools for Note-Taking

Modern technology offers numerous tools to enhance note-taking:

Examples

Microsoft OneNote, Evernote, Google Keep.

Advantages

- Cloud-based storage for easy access and backup.
- Ability to integrate multimedia elements (images, videos, links).
- Easy editing and organization.

Disadvantages

- Dependence on technology and internet access.
- Potential distractions from other applications.

5. Reviewing and Revising Notes

Taking notes is only the first step; regular review and revision are crucial for long-term retention and understanding.

Importance of Reviewing

- Reinforces learning by revisiting the material.
- Identifies gaps or areas requiring clarification.

Revision Strategies

- Review notes within 24 hours of taking them.
- Use the Cornell Method's summary section to test recall.
- Collaborate with classmates to compare and expand understanding.
- Employ color-coding to highlight key points during revision.

6. Common Pitfalls in Note-Taking

Avoid these common mistakes to ensure effective note-taking:

a) Overloading

Attempting to record every word can lead to incomplete understanding and inefficient notes.

b) Disorganization

Unstructured notes are harder to review and may hinder retention.

c) Passive Engagement

Failing to stay focused results in incomplete or inaccurate notes.

d) Neglecting Review

Notes left unreviewed are less likely to aid long-term learning.

Conclusion

Effective note-taking is both an art and a science, integral to academic success. By understanding and practicing various techniques, such as the Cornell Method, mind mapping, and charting, students can organize, retain, and apply information more effectively. Consistent practice, active engagement, and adaptability to individual learning styles are essential to mastering this critical skill.

Questions

1. Define note-taking and explain its importance in academic and professional settings.
2. Discuss the different types of note-taking methods, such as the Cornell Method, Mind.

   Mapping, and Charting. Provide examples of when each might be most effective.
3. How does effective note-taking contribute to better comprehension and retention of information? Explain with examples.
4. What are the key challenges people face in note-taking, and how can they overcome these challenges?
5. What is the Cornell Note-Taking Method, and how does it differ from traditional note-taking techniques?

6. Describe the structure of a Cornell note sheet. What are the specific functions of the key areas: the Notes Column, Cue Column, and Summary Section?
7. Explain how the Cornell Method can help in organizing and reviewing notes effectively.
8. What types of content or scenarios are best suited for using the Cornell Note-Taking Method? Provide examples.
9. What are the key elements of an effective note? Illustrate your answer with examples.
10. Discuss how abbreviations, symbols, and shorthand can make note-taking more efficient. Provide examples of commonly used abbreviations and symbols.

9

Oral Presentation

Objectives

- To understand the fundamental elements of preparing and delivering an effective oral presentation.
- To explore techniques for organizing content logically and engaging the audience effectively.
- To learn practical tips for improving articulation, delivery, and body language during presentations.
- To identify strategies for using visual aids and technology to enhance presentations.
- To develop confidence and professionalism in diverse public speaking scenarios.

Introduction

Oral presentations are an integral part of professional domains, including business, technical, scientific, industrial, and managerial fields. They involve delivering specialized information on a specific topic to a relatively small yet knowledgeable audience. As a student, you may present findings from advanced studies, research, or project proposals to peers and teachers. As a professional, you might present technical, business, or scientific data to colleagues, explain policy changes to employees, or deliver papers at conferences and seminars. The need for oral presentations grows as one progresses in their career, making it essential to hone these skills early.

Planning and Preparation

- Effective preparation is key to a successful presentation. Begin by
- Identifying the purpose, audience, and time constraints.
- Gathering material from reliable sources.
- Preparing note cards with key points, quotations, or anecdotes for greater impact.

If using visual aids like PowerPoint slides, ensure they align with your notes and are sequentially numbered. This helps maintain focus on the topic while enabling eye contact with the audience.

Practice and Rehearsal

Practice is essential for building confidence and eliminating nervousness. Rehearse in a realistic setup with audio-visual aids and, if possible, before friends or peers to receive constructive feedback.

Articulation and Delivery

Before speaking, ensure:

- Note cards and slides are well-organized.
- You are appropriately dressed for the occasion.
- The venue's technical arrangements are suitable.

During Delivery

- Speak extemporaneously for a professional tone.
- Pronounce words clearly with proper intonation.
- Maintain eye contact and avoid excessive reliance on visuals.

Choice of Words

Use clear, plain language with short, familiar words to make your message easily understandable. Avoid clichés and overused expressions to maintain authenticity.

Managing Jargon

Use jargon sparingly and only when the audience is familiar with the technical terms. For mixed audiences, replace jargon with plain terms to ensure clarity.

Sentence Construction

Construct short, simple sentences to maintain the audience's focus. Avoid monotony by varying expressions and using conversational language to keep the presentation engaging.

Visual Aids

Choose visual aids that suit the audience size, seating arrangement, and venue facilities. Ensure illustrations are neat, uncluttered, and emphasize key points. While presenting visuals:

- Keep them visible to the entire audience.
- Avoid blocking the display.
- Reference visuals only when discussing them.

Evaluating Oral Presentations

Use the following criteria to evaluate a presentation effectively:

Introduction to the topic

Clarity and sequence of presentation. Voice modulation and delivery.

Use of visual aids.

Interaction with the audience. Knowledge of the subject.

Style of conclusion.

Evaluation Sheet for Oral Presentation

Name of the Presenter: ______________________________

Date of Presentation: ______________________________

Rate each category on a scale of 1 (Poor) to 5 (Excellent):

a. Introduction to the topic: _____________
b. Clarity of presentation: _____________
c. Sequence and continuity: _____________
d. Voice, pitch, and delivery: _____________
e. Use of visual aids: _____________
f. Eye contact and audience awareness: _____________
g. Interaction with the audience: _____________
h. General poise and bearing: _____________
i. Knowledge of the subject: _____________
j. Style of conclusion: _____________

Total Score: _____________

Remarks (if any): .

Signature: _____________

Questions

1. What are the key elements to consider when preparing an oral presentation?
2. How can you effectively engage your audience during an oral presentation?
3. What are the common mistakes to avoid during an oral presentation, and how can they be corrected?
4. How does body language influence the effectiveness of an oral presentation?
5. What strategies can be used to handle nervousness or anxiety before and during an oral presentation?
6. How can visual aids (like slides) enhance or hinder the delivery of an oral presentation?

10

English Sounds: Word Stress, Intonation, Patterns, and Composition

Objectives

- To explore the significance of word stress and its impact on pronunciation and meaning.
- To examine the role of intonation in conveying emotions, questions, and statements.
- To analyze different speech patterns in English and their practical applications.
- To discuss the composition of sounds in English, including vowel and consonant sounds, and how they form speech.
- To enhance students' listening, speaking, and pronunciation skills through a deeper understanding of sound dynamics.

Introduction

The study of English sounds involves understanding how words are pronounced, the patterns they follow, and how these elements affect communication. Mastering the intricacies of word stress, intonation, and speech patterns enhances a speaker's ability to communicate effectively and clearly in English. These components play a crucial role in conveying not just the literal meaning but also the speaker's intent and emotions.

Overview of English Sounds

English sounds can be broadly categorized into vowels, consonants, and semi-vowels. Understanding these foundational elements is crucial before diving into stress, intonation, and pattern composition.

- **Vowel Sounds:** Produced without significant constriction of airflow, vowels are the backbone of syllables in English. There are both short and long vowels, diphthongs (combination of two vowels), and triphthongs (combination of three vowels).

- **Consonant Sounds:** Produced by obstructing airflow in some way, consonants include voiced and voiceless sounds. Consonants can be classified based on place and manner of articulation, such as plosives, fricatives, nasals, and affricates.
- **Phonetic Transcription:** A tool used to represent sounds, helping learners understand pronunciation irrespective of spelling.

Word Stress

Word stress refers to the emphasis placed on a particular syllable within a word. Stress patterns can alter the meaning and part of speech of words, making it a critical aspect of pronunciation.

Primary Stress vs. Secondary Stress: Primary stress is the strongest emphasis in a word, while secondary stress is less prominent.

Rules of Word Stress:

- **Two-Syllable Words:** For nouns and adjectives, stress typically falls on the first syllable (e.g., 'TAble', 'HAPpy'). For verbs, it usually falls on the second syllable (e.g., 'beGIN', 'deCIDE').
- **Three-Syllable Words:** The stress often depends on the suffix and the type of word. Common patterns include stressing the first or second syllable.
- **Compound Words:** Stress usually falls on the first part of compound nouns (e.g., 'BLACKboard') but can vary in adjectives and verbs (e.g., 'old- FAshioned').

Impact on Meaning: Incorrect word stress can lead to misunderstandings, as it can change the meaning of words (e.g., 'REcord' (noun) vs. 'reCORD' (verb)).

Intonation in English

Intonation refers to the rise and fall of pitch in speech, which plays a crucial role in conveying meaning beyond the literal words spoken. It affects how messages are interpreted, indicating questions, statements, emotions, and more.

Types of Intonation Patterns

- **Rising Intonation:** Commonly used in yes/no questions (e.g., "Are you coming?") and shows uncertainty or incompleteness.
- **Falling Intonation:** Indicates finality and is used in statements, commands, and Wh- questions (e.g., "Where are you going?").

- **Rising-Falling Intonation:** Expresses surprise, disbelief, or emphasis (e.g., "Really!").
- **Level Intonation:** Often used in monotone or when listing items without much variation in pitch.

Functions of Intonation

- **Grammatical Function:** Distinguishes questions from statements (e.g., "You're coming." vs. "You're coming?").
- **Attitudinal Function:** Reflects the speaker's emotions, such as happiness, sadness, anger, or sarcasm.
- **Discourse Function:** Helps in maintaining the flow of conversation, indicating when a speaker has finished or wants to continue speaking.

Patterns in English Speech

Speech patterns refer to the way sounds, stress, and intonation work together in English. Understanding these patterns helps in fluent speaking and effective communication.

1. **Rhythm and Stress-Timed Language:** English is considered a stress-timed language, where stressed syllables occur at regular intervals, making the rhythm an essential part of speech.
2. **Connected Speech:** In natural speech, words are often linked together, and sounds can be modified or even dropped. Key aspects include:
   a) **Elision:** The omission of sounds in connected speech (e.g., "next day" pronounced as /neks deɪ/).
   b) **Assimilation:** The process where a sound changes due to the influence of neighboring sounds (e.g., "input" pronounced as /ɪmpʊt/).
   c) **Linking:** Smooth transitions between words, often blending sounds to maintain the flow (e.g., "an apple" pronounced as /ənæpl/).

Intonation Patterns in Conversational English: These patterns include statements, questions, commands, and exclamations, all influenced by intonation.

Composition of English Sounds

The composition of sounds involves understanding how vowels, consonants, and their combinations create words and how these words interact in speech.

- **Syllable Structure:** A syllable is a basic unit of speech composed of a vowel sound, with or without surrounding consonants (e.g., "cat" has one syllable, while "caterpillar" has four).

- **Phonotactics:** The rules governing the permissible combinations of sounds in a language, affecting how sounds are arranged within words.
- **Sound Blending:** The process of merging individual sounds to form words, crucial for developing reading and speaking skills in English.
- **Pronunciation Variations:** Differences in pronunciation based on dialect, accent, and regional influences affect sound composition and stress patterns.

Practical Applications of Sound Patterns in Communication

Understanding and mastering sound patterns, stress, and intonation greatly impact daily communication, particularly in academic and professional settings.

- **Enhancing Comprehension:** Proper use of stress and intonation helps in better understanding and interpreting spoken English.
- **Improving Speaking Skills:** Fluent speech, appropriate intonation, and correct stress patterns make communication more engaging and understandable.
- **Listening Skills Development:** Exposure to different intonation patterns helps in distinguishing between types of statements, questions, and emotions, improving overall listening comprehension.
- **Professional Contexts:** In presentations, interviews, and public speaking, mastering these aspects of English sounds helps convey confidence and clarity.

Challenges in Mastering English Sounds

- **Variability in English Accents:** Differences in regional accents can affect pronunciation and comprehension of sound patterns.
- **Influence of Native Language:** Native language interference often affects the acquisition of English sounds, leading to pronunciation errors.
- **Inconsistent Spelling and Pronunciation:** English's inconsistent spelling rules create challenges in predicting correct pronunciation and stress placement.

Strategies for Improving Sound Mastery

- **Phonetic Practice:** Regular practice with phonetic transcriptions can aid in mastering pronunciation.

- **Listening Exercises:** Engaging with varied English audio materials like podcasts, movies, and conversations helps in recognizing different sound patterns.
- **Speech Shadowing:** Mimicking native speakers' pronunciation, intonation, and rhythm helps in naturalizing speech patterns.
- **Use of Language Learning Apps:** Tools like Duolingo, ELSA Speak, and YouTube tutorials focus specifically on pronunciation, stress, and intonation improvement.

Understanding the nuances of English sounds, including word stress, intonation, and speech patterns, is vital for effective communication. Mastery of these elements enhances not only pronunciation but also the ability to convey meaning and emotion, making communication in English clearer and more impactful.

Questions

1. Define word stress and explain its importance in English pronunciation. Provide examples of how stress changes the meaning of words.
2. Describe the types of intonation patterns and their functions in English communication.
3. Explain the concept of connected speech and provide examples of elision, assimilation, and linking.
4. How do speech patterns affect communication in English? Discuss the importance of rhythm and stress-timed language.
5. What are the challenges faced by English learners in mastering sound patterns and intonation? Suggest strategies to overcome these challenges.
6. Discuss the composition of English sounds. How do syllable structure and phonotactics influence word formation?
7. Why is intonation important in professional and academic settings? Provide examples of its impact on communication.
8. How can native language influence affect the pronunciation of English sounds?

   Provide examples of common errors and ways to address them.
9. Identify and explain strategies for improving pronunciation and mastery of English sounds.

11

Consonant Sounds with Symbols and Pronunciation

Objectives

- Provide a comprehensive understanding of consonant sounds in English.
- Familiarize learners with the International Phonetic Alphabet (IPA) symbols for consonant sounds.
- Enhance pronunciation skills through the correct articulation of consonant sounds.
- Enable learners to distinguish between voiced and voiceless consonants
- Equip learners with practical examples to apply phonetic knowledge in speaking and listening effectively.

Introduction

Consonant sounds are an integral part of spoken English, contributing significantly to the clarity and intelligibility of speech. Unlike vowel sounds, consonants are produced with a degree of constriction or closure in the vocal tract, which modifies the airflow. These sounds can be categorized based on various parameters, such as their place of articulation, manner of articulation, and whether they are voiced or voiceless.

The International Phonetic Alphabet (IPA) provides a standardized set of symbols to represent these sounds, ensuring a consistent approach to learning pronunciation. Understanding consonant sounds and their IPA symbols allows learners to decode and produce words accurately, improving their overall communication skills.

This section will explore the 24 consonant sounds of English, their IPA symbols, and pronunciation techniques. Additionally, it will provide examples and exercises to practice and master these sounds. By the end of this module, learners will have a solid foundation in consonant sounds, enabling them to speak English with confidence and precision.

Consonant Sounds with Symbols and Pronunciation

Sound Symbol	Sound Description	Pronunciation in Hindi	Example Word	Example in Hindi
/p/	Voiceless bilabial plosive	प (as in "पतंग")	pen	पेन
/b/	Voiced bilabial plosive	ब (as in "बतख")	bat	बैट
/t/	Voicelessa	ट (as in "टोकरी")	tap	टैप
/d/	Voiced alv eolar plosive	ड (as in "डाक")	dog	डॉग
/k/	Voiceless velar plosive	क (as in "कमल")	cat	कैट
/g/	Voiced vel ar plosive	ग (as in "गमला")	go	गो
/f/	Voiceless labiodental fricative	फ (as in "फल")	fan	फैन
/v/	Voiced labiodental fricative	व (as in "वन")	van	वैन
/θ/	Voiceless dental fricative	थ (soft "थ" as in "थकान")	think	थिंक
/δ/	Voiced dental fricative	ध (as in "धन")	this	दिस
/s/	Voiceless alveolar fricative	स (as in "समय")	sit	सिट
/d_3/	Voiced alveolar fricative	ज़ (as in "ज़हर")	zoo	ज़ू
/M/	Voiceless postalveolar fricative	श (as in "शेर")	ship	शिप
/3/	Voiced postalveolar fricative	झ (as in "झुंड")	measure	मेज़र
/tʃ/	Voiceless postalveolar affricate	च (as in "चाय")	chip	चिप
w	Voiced postalveolar affricate	ज (as in "जग")	jam	जैम

/m/	Voiced bilabial nasal	म (as in " मछली")	man	मैन
/n/	Voiced alveolar nasal	न (as in "नमक")	nap	नैप
/η/	Voiced velar nasal	ड़ (as in "कंगन")	leg	लेग
/I/	Voiced alveolar lateral	ल (as in "लालटेन")	leg	लग
/r/	Voiced alveolar approximant	र (as in "रंग")	red	रेड
/J/	Voiced palatal approximant	य (as in "यम")	yes	यस
/w/	Voiced labio-velar approximant	व (as in "वक्त")	wet	वेट
/h/	Voiceless glottal fricative	ह (as in "हाथी")	hat	हैट

Vowel Sounds with Symbols and Pronunciation (English to Hindi)

Sound Symbol	**Sound Description**	**Pronunciation in Hindi**	**Example Word**	**Example in Hindi**
/i:/	Long high front vowel	ई (as in "सी")	see	सी
/I/	Short high front vowel	ई (as in "बिल")	sit	सिट
/e/	Mid front vowel	ई (as in "कहानी"	bed	बेड
/ae/	Low front vowel	ई (as in "बैठक")	cat	कैट
/ɑ:/	Long low back vowel	ई (as in "राम")	car	कार
/ɒ:/	Short low back vowel	ई (as in "कॉन")	hot	हॉट
/o:/	Long mid back rounded vowel	ई (as in "रोम")	saw	सॉ
/o/		ई(as in "उम्मीद")	put	पुट
/u:/	Long high back rounded vowel	ई (as in "झूला")	food	फूड
/ʌ/	Central vowel	ई (as in "अधिकार")	cup	कप
/e/	Schwa (mid central vowel)	ई (as in "गरीब")	about	अबाउट
/ɜ:/	Long mid-central vowel	ई (as in "बहुत")	bird	बर्ड
/əʊ/	Diphthong sound	(as in "नौक")	go	गो

Diphthongs Chart with Hindi Equivalents

Sound Symbol	Sound of Fescription	Pronunciation in Hindi	Example Word	Example in Hindi
/eɪ/	Combination of /e/ and /ɪ/	एई (as in "बेटे")	day	डे
/aɪ/	Combination of /a/ and /ɪ/	आइ (as in "आई")	my	माई
/ɔɪ/	Combination of /ɪ/ and /ɪ/	ऑइ (as in "आइल")	boy	बॉय
/aʊ/	Combination of /a/ and /ʊ/	आउ (as in "काऊ")	now	नाउ
/əʊ/	Combination of /ə/ and /ʊ/	औ (as in "मौसमी")	go	गो
/ɪə/	Combination of /ɪ/ and /ə/	इअ (as in "मीडिया")	near	नियर
/eə/	Combination of /e/ and /ə/	एअ (as in "टेलर")	air	एयर
/ʊə/	Combination of /ə/ and /ə/	उअ (as in "गुआ")	tour	टूर

List of Significant Words with Stress Marks

1. **OBject (noun) – OB-ject**

   Meaning: An item or thing.

   Example: The mysterious object was found on the beach.

2. **PROduce (noun) – PRO-duce**

   Meaning: Fruits and vegetables.

   Example: The market sells fresh produce.

3. **PERmit (noun) – PER-mit** Meaning: An official authorization. Example: You need a permit to park here.

4. **REfuse (noun) – RE-fuse**

   Meaning: Waste or trash.

   Example: The bins were full of refuse.

5. **INcrease (noun) – IN-crease**

   Meaning: A rise or growth.

   Example: There was a significant increase in sales.

6. **EXport (noun) – EX-port** Meaning: Goods sent out of a country. Example: Oil is the country's main export.

7. **IMport (noun) – IM-port**

   Meaning: Goods brought into a country.

   Example: The import of luxury cars has increased.

8. **SUBject (noun) – SUB-ject** Meaning: A topic or area of study. Example: Mathematics is her favorite subject.

9. **CONvert (noun) – CON-vert** Meaning: Someone who changes beliefs. Example: He is a recent convert to vegetarianism.
10. **CONtest (noun) – CON-test**

    Meaning: A competition.

    Example: She won the baking contest.
11. **REject (noun) – RE-ject**

    Meaning: Something discarded.

    Example: The product was a reject due to a defect.
12. **INSult (noun) – IN-sult**

    Meaning: An offensive remark.

    Example: She took his words as an insult.
13. **PERfect (adjective) – PER-fect**

    Meaning: Flawless.

    Example: Her performance was perfect.
14. **DEcrease (noun) – DE-crease**

    Meaning: A reduction.

    Example: The decrease in temperature was sudden.
15. **PROtest (noun) – PRO-test**

    Meaning: A demonstration.Example: There was a protest against the new law
16. **obJECT (verb) – ob-JECT** Meaning: To oppose or disagree. Example: She objected to the proposal.
17. **proDUCE (verb) – pro-DUCE** Meaning: To create or manufacture. Example: The factory produces high-quality goods.
18. **perMIT (verb) – per-MIT**

    Meaning: To allow or grant.

    Example: The manager did not permit the changes.
19. **reFUSE (verb) – re-FUSE** Meaning: To decline or reject. Example: He refused the offer.
20. **inCREASE (verb) – in-CREASE** Meaning: To become larger or greater. Example: Prices are expected to increase next year.
21. **exPORT (verb) – ex-PORT**

    Meaning: To send goods abroad.

    Example: They export electronics to Europe.

22. **imPORT (verb) – im-PORT** Meaning: To bring in goods from abroad. Example: The company imports raw materials from Asia.
23. **subJECT (verb) – sub-JECT** Meaning: To undergo or experience. Example: The proposal was subjected to scrutiny.
24. **conVERT (verb) – con-VERT** Meaning: To change or transform. Example: They plan to convert the old factory into apartments.
25. **conTEST (verb) – con-TEST** Meaning: To challenge or dispute. Example: They contested the results of the election.
26. **reJECT (verb) – re-JECT** Meaning: To refuse or turn down. Example: The committee rejected his application.
27. **inSULT (verb) – in-SULT** Meaning: To offend or speak disrespectfully.

    Example: He insulted his colleague during the meeting
28. **CONsole (noun) – CON-sole** Meaning: A control panel or device. Example: The gaming console is popular among teens.
29. **ADdress (noun) – AD-dress** Meaning: A location or place where someone lives or works.

    Example: I wrote down her address.
30. **CONduct (noun) – CON-duct** Meaning: Behavior or manner of acting. Example: His conduct was exemplary.
31. **CONflict (noun) – CON-flict**

    Meaning: A serious disagreement or argument.

    Example: The conflict between them is unresolved.
32. **DESert (noun) – DES-ert**

    Meaning: A barren land, typically sandy or dry.

    Example: The Sahara is a vast desert.
33. **INsult (noun) – IN-sult** Meaning: A disrespectful or scornful remark.

    Example: She took his comment as an insult.
34. **PERmit (noun) – PER-mit**

    Meaning: An official document that allows you to do something.

    Example: You need a permit to park here.
35. **PROject (noun) – PRO-ject** Meaning: A planned undertaking, often in education or business.
36. **perFECT (verb) – per-FECT** Meaning: To make something flawless. Example: She worked hard to perfect her skills.

37. **deCREASE (verb) – de-CREASE** Meaning: To reduce or become less. Example: They plan to decrease expenses this year.
38. **proTEST (verb) – pro-TEST** Meaning: To express objection. Example: Citizens protested against the policy.
39. **conSOLE (verb) – con-SOLE**

    Meaning: To comfort someone.

    Example: She tried to console him after his loss.
40. **adDRESS (verb) – ad-DRESS**

    Meaning: To speak to someone or handle a problem.

    Example: He will address the crowd tomorrow.
41. **conDUCT (verb) – con-DUCT**

    Meaning: To lead or guide something, such as an experiment or meeting.

    Example: She will conduct the survey.
42. **conFLICT (verb) – con-FLICT**

    Meaning: To clash or be incompatible. Example: Their interests conflict with ours.
43. **deSERT (verb) – de-SERT**

    Meaning: To abandon someone or something.

    Example: He deserted his post.
44. **inSULT (verb) – in-SULT**

    Meaning: To offend someone by disrespect.

    Example: Don't insult your colleagues.
45. **perMIT (verb) – per-MIT**

    Meaning: To allow something to happen.

    Example: He doesn't permit smoking inside.
46. **proJECT (verb) – pro-JECT**

    Meaning: To estimate or forecast something based.
47. **REcord (noun)** – RE-cord Meaning: A documented piece of information, often kept for future reference Example: Keep a record of your expenses.
48. **reCORD (verb)** – re-CORD **Meaning:** To capture or document information, sounds, or images **Example:** Please record the meeting.
49. **OBject (noun)** – OB-ject **Meaning:** A tangible item or thing. **Example:** He picked up the shiny object.

50. **obJECT (verb)** – ob-JECT

    Meaning: To express disagreement or disapproval.

    Example: She objected to the decision.

51. **EXport (noun)** – EX-port

    Meaning: Goods sent to another country for sale.

    Example: The country's main export is oil.

52. **exPORT (verb)** – ex-PORT **Meaning:** To send goods abroad **Example:** They export cars to Europe.

53. **IMport (noun)** – IM-port

    Meaning: Goods brought into a country from abroad.

    Example: Imports have increased this year.

54. **imPORT (verb)** – im-PORT **Meaning:** To bring in goods from another country

    Example: They import electronics from Japan.

55. **UPdate (noun)** – UP-date **Meaning:** A new version or improved information.

    Example: Check for software updates regularly.

56. **upDATE (verb)** – up-DATE **Meaning:** To bring up to date by adding new information.

    Example: I need to update my profile.

57. **CONtract (noun)** – CON-tract **Meaning:** A legal agreement between two or more parties.

    Example: They signed the contract.

58. **conTRACT (verb)** – con-TRACT **Meaning:** To make something smaller or shorter.

    Example: Muscles contract when exercising.

59. **REsearch (noun)** – RE-search **Meaning:** Systematic investigation or study **Example:** His research is groundbreaking.

60. **reSEARCH (verb)** – re-SEARCH **Meaning:** To study or investigate systematically.

    Example: They are researching new technologies.

61. **UPset (noun)** – UP-set.

    Meaning: A state of being emotionally disturbed.

    Example: There was an upset in the game.

62. **upSET (verb)** – up-SET

    Meaning: To disturb or overturn.

    Example: The news upset her greatly.

63. **INvite (noun)**

    Meaning: A written or spoken request for someone to go somewhere.

    Example: I received an invite.

64. **inVITE (verb) – in-VITE**

    Meaning: To ask someone to attend or come to an event.

    Example: They invited us to the party.

Questions

1. Differentiate between voiced and voiceless consonants. Give three examples of each.
1. Define what a syllable is. What are its components?
2. Break the following words into their syllabic structure:

   a) Computer b) Elephant

   c) Butterfly
3. Explain what word stress is and why it is significant in English.
4. Mark the stress pattern of the following words:

   a) Photograph b) Democracy

   c) Information
5. What is intonation, and how does it affect the meaning of a sentence?
6. Provide examples of how intonation can change the meaning in the following sentences:

   a) "You're coming." b) "You're coming?"
7. What are minimal pairs? Give three examples of minimal pairs in English.
8. How do minimal pairs help in improving pronunciation?
9. Define a diphthong. Can you list some common diphthongs in English?
10. Transcribe the following words that contain diphthongs:

    a) Coin b) House

    c) Ride

11. What is phonemic awareness, and how does it contribute to language learning?
12. Create a list of words that start with the same phoneme and explain how this can aid in phonemic awareness.
13. How can understanding sound symbols improve your spoken English?
14. Listen to a short audio clip of spoken English. Write down any words that you find challenging to transcribe phonetically and explain why they are challenging.
15. Create a phonetic symbols chart that includes at least 20 symbols with their corresponding sounds and example words. Present it to the class.
16. What is phonetic transcription, and why is it important in understanding pronunciation?
17. Transcribe the following words using phonetic symbols:

    a) Cat   b) Fish
18. What does IPA stand for? Describe its purpose.
19. Provide the IPA symbols for the following sounds:

    a) The voiceless plosive /p/   b) The voiced fricative /v/
20. Identify and list the five vowel sounds in English. Provide an example word for each.

12

Writing Skills

Objectives

- Understand the concepts of precise writing, abstracting, and summarizing.
- Develop skills for condensing complex information effectively.
- Learn the essentials of the style of technical communication.
- Apply these writing techniques in various professional and academic settings.

Writing Skills

Writing skills, particularly in the professional and academic environment, are essential for communicating complex ideas clearly and concisely. Three important forms of condensing information are **precise writing, abstracting, and summarizing**, each serving a distinct purpose in effective communication. Alongside these, the **style of technical communication** plays a crucial role in ensuring that the information is communicated in a clear, structured, and efficient manner.

Precise Writing

Precise writing involves shortening a lengthy passage or document by conveying the core message without losing essential meaning. It requires understanding the main ideas, removing unnecessary details, and reconstructing the text in a concise form.

Characteristics of Precise Writing

- **Clarity:** The text must clearly reflect the original idea.
- **Brevity:** Only the key points are retained, cutting out redundant or elaborate expressions.
- **Cohesion:** The rephrased content should flow logically and maintain the essence of the original.
- **Objectivity:** Precise writing eliminates personal opinions or interpretations that weren't in the original text.

Steps in Writing a Precise

S. No.	Steps	Description
1.	Reading Comprehensively	Understand the entire text thoroughly before trying to shorten or rewrite it.
2.	Identify the Key Points	Extract only the essential ideas. Skip examples, repetition, and extra details.
3.	Rephrase Concisely	Rewrite the main points in your own words using fewer words without changing the meaning.
4.	Review and Edit	Ensure that the summary reflects the original message accurately and clearly

Example of Precise Writing

Original Text

Communication is an essential skill in all areas of life, whether it's in the workplace, in personal relationships, or in social settings. Good communication fosters better understanding, increases productivity, and helps in resolving conflicts effectively.

Precise

Effective communication is vital for understanding, productivity, and conflict resolution in all life domains.

Abstracting

Abstracting refers to the process of creating a concise summary of a longer text, specifically used to summarize research articles, papers, or reports. An abstract captures the key points, methodology, findings, and conclusion in a brief paragraph, allowing readers to quickly understand the content of a document without reading the entire text.

Types of Abstracts Descriptive Abstract: Briefly describes the content and structure of the document but doesn't provide any detailed findings or conclusions.

Informative Abstract: Provides a comprehensive summary of the main ideas, methods, results, and conclusions of the text.

Structure of an Abstract

1. **Introduction:** Context or background of the research.
2. **Objective:** The purpose or aim of the study.
3. **Methods:** A brief description of how the research was conducted.

4. **Results:** A summary of the main findings.
5. **Conclusion:** Final thoughts or implications of the study.

Writing an Effective Abstract

- **Be concise:** Avoid elaboration; focus on key points.
- **Stay objective:** Present the facts and results without personal opinions.
- **Use simple language:** Ensure clarity, avoiding technical jargon unless absolutely necessary.
- **Follow the structure:** Maintain a logical flow from introduction to conclusion.

Example of an Informative Abstract

Original Article

"This study investigates the effects of workplace communication on employee performance. A survey was conducted with 200 participants across five industries. The results show that effective communication significantly enhances employee productivity and job satisfaction. Recommendations for improving communication practices are also discussed."

Informative Abstract

"This research examines the impact of communication on employee performance in various industries. Survey results from 200 participants indicate that effective workplace communication improves productivity and job satisfaction. The study concludes with recommendations for better communication practices."

Summarizing

Summarizing involves condensing a longer text or passage into a short version by capturing the main ideas and presenting them in a brief format. Unlike precise writing, which focuses on cutting down word count while retaining meaning, summarizing is concerned with the overall gist of the original text.

Key Features of Summarizing

- **Conciseness:** The goal is to reduce the text to its essential points.
- **Relevance:** Only key ideas and facts are retained.
- **Objectivity:** Personal opinions or interpretations are avoided.
- **Simplicity:** The summary must be easy to understand for the reader.

Techniques for Effective Summarizing

1. **Skimming the Text:** Identify the main themes and headings.
2. **Highlighting Key Ideas:** Focus on the main arguments or points presented.
3. **Condensing Information:** Use fewer words to communicate the central points without unnecessary details.
4. **Reviewing:** Ensure the summary accurately represents the original text's meaning.

Example of Summarizing

Original Passage

"Digital communication tools have revolutionized the workplace by allowing employees to collaborate in real-time from different locations. However, they also present challenges such as information overload and misinterpretation of messages, which can hinder productivity."

Digital tools enhance workplace collaboration but can lead to challenges like infor mation overload and miscommunication.

Questions

- What is the difference between summarizing, abstracting, and precise writing? Provide examples for each.
- What are the key steps involved in writing a precise?
- How does summarizing help in understanding and condensing complex information?
- What is the structure of an informative abstract, and how does it differ from a descriptive abstract?
- Why is objectivity important in both summarizing and precise writing?
- Explain the role of context in precise writing. How do you ensure that the main idea is retained?
- What are the common mistakes to avoid while writing a summary or abstract?
- Describehowreadingcomprehensionplaysaroleineffectivesummarizing.
- How can precise writing be useful in academic and professional settings? Provide an example.
- When should you use an abstract instead of a summary, and why?

13

Style of Technical Communication

The **style of technical communication** focuses on delivering information clearly, concisely, and accurately, often in a professional or academic context. Technical communication is typically used in fields such as science, engineering, technology, and medicine to convey complex data or instructions to a specific audience.

Characteristics of Technical Communication Style

- **Clarity:** The message should be easy to understand without ambiguity.
- **Conciseness:** Information is conveyed using as few words as necessary.
- **Accuracy:** The content must be precise and free from errors, especially when explaining technical data.
- **Objectivity:** The style is factual and free from personal bias or opinions.
- **Consistency:** Terminology, units of measurement, and formatting should remain consistent throughout the document.

Types of Technical Communication

- **Instructions/Manuals:** Step-by-step guides for completing a task or operating machinery.
- **Reports:** Detailed documentation of findings or research.
- **Proposals:** Formal suggestions for a project or plan.
- **Emails/Business Letters:** Professional correspondence.
- **Presentations:** Visual and oral methods of conveying technical information.

Common Formats in Technical Communication

- **Standardized Structure:** Many technical documents follow a strict format, such as reports with headings like Introduction, Methods, Results, and Conclusion.
- **Use of Visual Aids:** Charts, graphs, and diagrams are often used to simplify complex data.

- **Bullet Points and Numbering:** These tools are frequently used to list points in a clear and organized manner.

Differences between Technical and General Writing

Aspect	Technical Writing	General Writing
Purpose	Inform, instruct, or explain	Entertain, express, or persuade
Audience	Experts or professionals in a field	General public or a wide audience
Style	Formal, objective, and concise	Can be informal, creative, and subjective
Use of Terminology	Specialized, technical vocabulary	Simple, everyday language
Structure	Structured with specific formats	Flexible structure, often narrative-based

Importance of Writing Skills in Technical Communication

- **Effective Knowledge Transfer:** Writing skills ensure that complex information is transmitted clearly to the intended audience.
- **Increased Productivity:** Well-written documents help save time by reducing the need for clarification.
- **Enhanced Professionalism:** Clear, concise, and error-free communication demonstrates professionalism in technical fields.
- **Minimized Misinterpretation:** Precise language in technical documents reduces the chances of misunderstandings.

Mastering writing skills such as precise writing, abstracting, and summarizing is critical for effective communication in both academic and professional contexts. These skills help condense complex information into a more digestible format without losing the essence of the message. Coupled with the style of technical communication, these techniques ensure that information is conveyed in a clear, concise, and accurate manner, especially in fields requiring precision and clarity.

Questions

- List and explain the key characteristics of effective technical communication.
- Why is clarity important in technical communication, and how can it be achieved?
- Describe the typical structure of a technical report.
- What role do visual aids (e.g., charts, graphs) play in technical communication?

- Explain the importance of audience analysis in technical communication.
- What are the common formats used in technical writing, and when should each be used?
- How does objectivity in tone and style contribute to the effectiveness of technical communication?
- What is the significance of consistency in terminology and formatting in technical documents?
- Provide an example of a technical communication document and explain its purpose and structure.

14

Innovative Methods to Enhance Vocabulary

Objectives

- To explore creative and interactive techniques for effective vocabulary expansion.
- To enhance understanding and retention of new words through context-based learning.
- To encourage the use of digital tools and apps for engaging vocabulary building.
- To promote collaborative learning strategies for vocabulary enhancement
- To develop critical thinking by applying new vocabulary in diverse contexts.

Contextual Learning

One of the most effective ways to learn new words is through **contextual learning**. This involves understanding words through the context in which they are used, rather than learning definitions in isolation.

Steps to Implement Contextual Learning

- **Reading Widely:** Expose yourself to a variety of texts (books, articles, blogs) to encounter new words in different contexts.
- **Word Journals:** Maintain a journal of new words with examples of how they are used in sentences.
- **Context Clues:** When encountering an unfamiliar word, try to deduce its meaning based on the surrounding words and context before looking it up.

Using Word Games and Puzzles

Gamification is a powerful tool to make learning vocabulary more interactive and fun. Word games and puzzles enhance retention and recall by engaging the brain in problem-solving activities.

Popular Word Games

- **Crossword Puzzles:** Help learners think about word meanings and synonyms.
- **Wordle:** A daily word-guessing game that stimulates critical thinking and vocabulary.
- **Scrabble:** Encourages creative thinking by forming words with limited letters.
- **Anagrams:** Involves rearranging letters to form new words, sharpening spelling and vocabulary skills.

Benefits of Word Games

- **Engagement:** Games create a sense of competition and motivation to improve vocabulary.
- **Repetition:** Repeated exposure to words through games strengthens memory.

Visual Vocabulary Learning

The use of **visual aids** like infographics, flashcards, and mind maps can enhance vocabulary retention, especially for visual learners. Associating words with images makes them easier to remember and recall.

Techniques for Visual Learning:

- **Flashcards:** Write the word on one side and its meaning or image on the other. Apps like Anki and Quizlet offer digital versions for easy practice.
- **Infographics:** Create or use existing infographics to visually connect words with their meanings, usage, and related terms.
- **Mind Maps:** Organize related words around a central concept, helping learners visualize connections between terms.

Learning through Technology and Apps

Modern technology offers a range of apps and tools that facilitate vocabulary building. These tools integrate learning into everyday life and often use spaced repetition techniques to aid memory retention.

Popular Vocabulary Apps

- **Duolingo:** Designed for language learners, it emphasizes vocabulary through interactive quizzes.
- **Memrise:** Focuses on vocabulary enhancement through spaced repetition and multimedia lessons.

- **Magoosh Vocabulary Builder:** Targets GRE and competitive exams, providing quizzes and word lists to improve vocabulary.

Advantages of Using Apps

- **Accessibility:** Learning can happen anytime, anywhere.
- **Personalization:** Apps tailor learning to individual levels, providing words based on user performance.

Root Words and Etymology

Understanding the **roots** of words helps in decoding unfamiliar terms and expands vocabulary exponentially. Root words, prefixes, and suffixes are the building blocks of many complex words in English.

Examples of Common Roots

- **Root: "bene" (Latin for good)**
  - Words: Benefit, Benevolent, Benefactor
- **Root: "chron" (Greek for time)**
  - Words: Chronology, Synchronize, Anachronism

Method

Study common roots and build word families around them. This helps in guessing the meaning of new words encountered.

Reading and Vocabulary Immersion

Frequent reading is one of the most natural ways to enhance vocabulary. Immersion in different genres of reading materials exposes learners to new words and their usage in context.

Techniques

- **Reading for Pleasure:** Explore different genres like fiction, non-fiction, newspapers, and academic journals.
- **Vocabulary Building Books:** Use books specifically designed to expand vocabulary, such as *Word Power Made Easy* by Norman Lewis.
- **Use Digital Readers:** Tools like Kindle offer built-in dictionaries that allow users to instantly look up unfamiliar words.

Using Mnemonics

Mnemonics are memory aids that help learners recall the meanings of words by associating them with patterns, images, or phrases.

Examples

- **Mnemonic for "Ostentatious" (showy or pretentious):**
  - Associate it with "Ostrich" (a big, attention-grabbing bird), and think of someone being as showy as an ostrich.
- **Mnemonic for "Ambidextrous" (able to use both hands equally well):**
  - "Ambi" means both, and "dextrous" means skillful, so imagine someone skillful with both hands.

Collaborative Learning: Vocabulary Circles

In group settings, **vocabulary circles** or discussion groups encourage collaborative learning. Students or participants are assigned specific words, and they present their understanding, use cases, and origins of the words to their peers.

Advantages of Vocabulary Circles

- **Active Engagement:** Group learning encourages active participation and deeper understanding.
- **Peer Learning:** Learners benefit from the collective knowledge of the group.

Monitoring Progress

To ensure vocabulary improvement, it's important to track progress and implement self- assessment techniques.

- **Quizzes and Tests:** Periodically test vocabulary to gauge improvement.
- **Writing Practice:** Use newly learned words in essays or discussions to reinforce their meanings.
- **Daily Practice:** Dedicate 10–15 minutes each day to vocabulary learning, using apps or word lists.

Expanding vocabulary is an ongoing process that requires consistent effort. By integrating innovative techniques like contextual learning, gamification, technology, and collaboration, learners can make vocabulary enhancement more enjoyable and effective. These methods not only help in memorizing new words but also in understanding their use in practical contexts, ultimately improving communication skills.

Questions

- What is contextual learning, and how does it help in enhancing vocabulary?
- List and explain three vocabulary apps that help improve vocabulary.
- How can word roots aid in understanding the meaning of unfamiliar words? Provide examples.
- What is the role of visual aids in learning vocabulary?
- Why is reading important for vocabulary building? Give two examples of reading techniques.
- How can mnemonic devices help in remembering difficult words? Provide an example.
- Describe how collaborative learning in vocabulary circles can enhance word retention.
- What is the difference between learning vocabulary through games and traditional methods? Which method do you prefer and why?

15

Analog, Its Structure and Types

Objectives

- Understand the concept and structure of analogy-based questions.
- Recognize different types of analogies used in reasoning.
- Develop strategies to approach analogy questions effectively.
- Enhance critical thinking and problem-solving skills through practice.

Introduction

An **analogy** is a comparison between two things that highlights a relationship or similarity between them. Analogical reasoning is frequently used in verbal reasoning sections of competitive exams, as well as in day-to-day problem-solving.

In analogy-based questions, pairs of words are given, and the goal is to identify the relationship between them and apply the same relationship to another pair. Analogies test your ability to comprehend relationships, draw logical inferences, and think critically.

Structure of an Analogy Question

Typically, an analogy question follows this format:

A : B :: C : D

This is read as "A is to B as C is to D." Your task is to identify the relationship between A and B and then find the word (D) that has the same relationship to C.

For example: **Dog : Puppy :: Cat : ?**

Here, "Dog" is related to "Puppy" as an adult animal is related to its young. Applying the same relationship, "Cat" would be related to "Kitten." Hence, the answer is "Kitten."

Types of Analogies

There are various types of analogies used in reasoning, and recognizing the category helps in solving analogy questions efficiently.

Synonym and Antonym Analogies

- **Synonym Analogy:** In this type, the two words in the pair are synonyms, meaning they have similar meanings.

  Example: **Big : Large :: Small : Tiny**
- **Antonym Analogy:** The words in the pair are opposites.

  Example: **Hot : Cold :: Tall : Short**

Part to Whole or Whole to Part Analogies

- **Part to Whole Analogy:** One word is a part of the other.
  - Example: **Finger : Hand :: Toe : Foot**
- **Whole to Part Analogy:** The relationship works in the reverse direction, where the second word is a part of the first.

  Example: **Tree : Leaf :: Car : Wheel**

Cause and Effect Analogies

These analogies highlight a relationship where one word causes the other.

Example: **Rain : Flood :: Fire : Burn**

Object and Function Analogies

In this type, one word is an object, and the other word refers to its function or purpose.

Example: **Pen : Write :: Knife : Cut**

Degree of Intensity Analogies

Here, the relationship is based on different levels of intensity between the two words.

Example: **Warm : Hot :: Cool : Cold**

Worker and Tool Analogies

This type of analogy relates a worker to the tool they use.

Example: **Painter : Brush :: Writer : Pen**

Object and Classification Analogies

One word is a specific instance, and the other is the general category it belongs to.

Example: **Dog : Mammal :: Sparrow : Bird**

Symbol and Representation Analogies

In this analogy, one word represents or symbolizes the other.

Example: **Heart : Love :: Dove : Peace**

How to Approach Analogies

When faced with an analogy question, follow these steps to solve it efficiently:

Step 1: Identify the Relationship

- Determine how the first pair of words (A and B) are related. Look for patterns like synonymy, cause-effect, part-whole, etc.

Step 2: Apply the Same Relationship

- Once the relationship is identified, look for the option that applies the same relationship to C and D.

Step 3: Eliminate Incorrect Options

- If you're unsure, eliminate options that don't fit the identified pattern. This increases your chances of choosing the correct answer.

Step 4: Practice

- Regular practice helps in recognizing patterns quickly. The more familiar you are with different types of relationships, the easier it will be to solve analogy questions.

Common Mistakes to Avoid

1. **Assuming the wrong relationship:** Often, two words may seem related in different ways, but only one relationship is correct for the analogy. Always double-check that the relationship fits the given pattern.
2. **Overcomplicating relationships:** Keep the relationship simple and straightforward.

   Complex reasoning may lead to unnecessary confusion.

3. **Ignoring subtle differences:** In analogy questions, slight differences in meaning can lead to incorrect choices. Pay attention to nuances in the words.
4. **Not considering all types of analogies:** Sometimes, the relationship isn't immediately obvious because it belongs to a less common category (e.g., symbolic relationships or degrees of intensity). Consider all possibilities before deciding.

Practice Questions

Exercise

Flower : Petal :: Book : ?

a) Page b) Cover

c) Word d) Chapter

Answer: a) Page Question 2

Doctor : Stethoscope :: Carpenter : ?

a) Hammer b) Saw

c) Nail d) Chisel

Answer: a) Hammer Question 3:

Sun : Day :: Moon : ?

a) Star b) Light

c) Night d) Sky

Answer: c) Night Question 4

Cow : Calf :: Horse : ?

a) Pony b) Foal

c) Colt d) Lamb

Answer: b) Foal Question 5

Write : Pen :: Paint : ?

a) Canvas b) Brush

c) Paper d) Color

Answer: b) Brush Question 6

Teacher : School :: Doctor : ?

a) Clinic b) Medicine

c) Health d) Surgery

Answer: a) Clinic Question 7

Tall : Short :: Heavy : ?

a) Thick b) Wide

c) Light d) Thin

Answer: c) Light Question 8

Fruit : Apple :: Vegetable : ?

a) Carrot b) Potato

c) Bread d) Meat

Answer: a) Carrot Question 9:

Bird : Wing :: Fish : ?

a) Water b) Fin

c) Scale d) Tail

Answer: b) Fin

Question 10:

Fire : Smoke :: Rain : ?

a) Water b) Cloud

c) Flood d) Storm

Answer: c) Flood

Analogy questions are a great way to test and enhance critical thinking and logical reasoning. They require a clear understanding of relationships between words, objects, or concepts. By practicing regularly and becoming familiar with different types of analogies, learners can significantly improve their ability to solve these questions accurately and efficiently.

Questions on Analogies with Answers

1. **Bird : Nest :: Fish : ?**

   a) Pond b) Aquarium

   c) Sea d) School

   Answer: b) Aquarium

2. **Tree : Forest :: Star : ?**

   a) Sky b) Galaxy

   c) Planet d) Universe

   Answer: b) Galaxy

3. **Hammer : Nail :: Screwdriver : ?**

   a) Bolt b) Screw

   c) Wrench d) Drill

   Answer: b) Screw

4. **Pencil : Write :: Eraser : ?**

   a) Draw b) Correct

   c) Color d) Erase

   Answer: d) Erase

5. **Book : Read :: Movie : ?**

   a) Watch b) See

   c) Review d) Direct

   Answer: a) Watch

6. **Doctor : Patient :: Teacher : ?**

   a) School b) Student

   c) Lesson d) Book

   Answer: b) Student

7. **Water : Ice :: Heat : ?**

   a) Cold b) Fire

   c) Steam d) Warmth

   Answer: c) Steam

8. **Heart : Pump :: Brain : ?**

a) Think
b) Calculate
c) Decide
d) Control

Answer: a) Think

9. **Cat : Kitten :: Dog : ?**

a) Puppy
b) Cub
c) Calf
d) Foal

Answer: a) Puppy

10. **Day : Night :: Summer : ?**

a) Winter
b) Fall
c) Spring
d) Rain

Answer: a) Winter

11. **Sword : Battle :: Pen : ?**

a) Write
b) Fight
c) Read
d) Draw

Answer: a) Write

12. **King : Kingdom :: Mayor : ?**

a) City
b) Town
c) Village
d) Country

Answer: a) City

13. **Sun : Day :: Moon : ?**

a) Night
b) Light
c) Star
d) Sky

Answer: a) Night

14. **Mountain : Hill :: Ocean : ?**

a) River
b) Lake
c) Pond
d) Stream

Answer: b) Lake

15. **Baby : Cradle :: Child : ?**

    a) Bed b) Chair

    c) Playground d) School

    Answer: c) Playground

16. **Brush : Paint :: Knife : ?**

    a) Cut b) Chop

    c) Spread d) Slice

    Answer: a) Cut

17. **Computer : Software :: Car : ?**

    a) Fuel b) Engine

    c) Mechanic d) Driver

    Answer: a) Fuel

18. **Lock : Key :: Question : ?**

    a) Answer b) Query

    c) Response d) Inquiry

    Answer: a) Answer

19. **Musician : Music :: Painter : ?**

    a) Paint b) Canvas

    c) Art d) Palette

    Answer: c) Art

20. **Salt : Ocean :: Sugar : ?**

    a) Candy b) Sweet

    c) Tea d) Dessert

    Answer: a) Candy

16

Study Material on Antecedents in Grammar

Objectives

- Understand the concept of antecedents in grammar and their role in sentence structure.
- Identify different types of antecedents and their functions in sentences.
- Recognize how antecedents relate to pronouns and other grammatical elements.
- Learn how to use antecedents correctly to avoid ambiguity and improve clarity in writing.
- Analyze examples of antecedents in various contexts to enhance comprehension and application.

Introduction

In grammar, an antecedent is a word or phrase that a pronoun refers back to in a sentence.

Antecedents are usually nouns or noun phrases that provide clarity about which person, place, thing, or idea is being discussed. The correct use of antecedents ensures that sentences are clear and that pronouns have specific references.

Types of Antecedents

Antecedents can be categorized into several types based on their nature:

- **Personal Antecedents:** These refer to specific people or things (e.g., *Alice* in "Alice loves her dog").
- **Impersonal Antecedents:** These refer to general concepts or groups (e.g., *Everyone* in "Everyone should do their best").
- **Collective Antecedents:** These refer to groups treated as a single unit (e.g., *The team* in "The team won its game").

- **Indefinite Antecedents:** These refer to non-specific persons or things (e.g., *Someone* in "Someone left their umbrella").

Relationship Between Antecedents and Pronouns

Pronouns are words that replace nouns or noun phrases. They must agree with their antecedents in number (singular or plural) and gender (masculine, feminine, or neuter). For example:

- Singular: "The cat is sleeping; it is tired." (*The pronoun "it" refers to the singular antecedent "cat".*)
- Plural: "The dogs are barking; they are hungry." (*The pronoun "they" refers to the plural antecedent "dogs".*)

Importance of Clarity and Avoiding Ambiguity

Using clear antecedents is essential for avoiding ambiguity in sentences. Ambiguous pronoun references can confuse readers. For example:

- Ambiguous: "When John spoke to Bob, he was angry." (*Who was angry: John or Bob?*)
- Clear: "When John spoke to Bob, John was angry." (*This clarifies that John was the one who was angry.*)

Examples and Practice

To reinforce understanding, here are some examples of antecedents in sentences:

- **Example 1:** "The teacher gave the students their assignments." (*"The teacher" is the antecedent for the pronoun "their".*)
- **Example 2:** "My brother and sister are visiting; they will arrive soon." (*"My brother and sister" is the antecedent for the pronoun "they".*)
- **Example 3:** "The committee reached its decision after a long debate." (*"The committee" is the antecedent for the pronoun "its".*)

Exercises for Practice

To reinforce your understanding of antecedents, consider the following exercises:

1. Identify the antecedent in the following sentence: "The dog chased its tail."
2. Rewrite the ambiguous sentence: "When Sarah met Julia, she smiled."
3. Provide a sentence using a collective antecedent and a corresponding pronoun.

4. Create a sentence with an indefinite antecedent and identify the pronoun that refers to it.

Communication Skills Terminology

1. **Sender**: The person or entity that initiates a message in the communication process.
2. **Receiver**: The person or entity to whom the message is directed or who receives the information.
3. **Message**: The information, idea, or thought that is being communicated from sender to receiver.
4. **Feedback**: The response or reaction from the receiver, indicating whether the message has been understood or needs clarification.
5. **Noise**: Any physical or psychological interference that distorts the clarity of the message being communicated. It can be external (environmental) or internal (emotional, mental).
6. **Channel**: The medium through which the message is transmitted, such as face-to-face conversation, email, phone call, or video chat.
7. **Context**: The environment, situation, or circumstances in which communication takes place, including the cultural, social, and physical factors.
8. **Non-verbal Communication**: Communication that occurs without the use of spoken or written language, relying on body language, gestures, facial expressions, posture, and eye contact.
9. **Paralanguage**: The non-verbal elements of communication, including tone of voice, pitch, volume, and intonation that accompany spoken language.
10. **Proxemics**: The study of how space and distance between people affect communication, including personal space and territoriality.
11. **Kinesics**: The study of body movements, gestures, and facial expressions as a form of communication.
12. **Perception**: The process by which individuals interpret and make sense of the stimuli they receive during communication.
13. **Emotional Intelligence (EI)**: The ability to understand and manage your own emotions, as well as recognize and influence the emotions of others in communication.
14. **Active Listening**: The practice of fully concentrating on, understanding, responding to, and remembering what the speaker says.

15. **Empathy**: The ability to understand and share the feelings of another person, which is crucial for effective interpersonal communication.
16. **Barriers to Communication**: Obstacles that prevent effective communication, including physical, psychological, emotional, and linguistic barriers.
17. **Contextual Communication**: Communication that is influenced by the situation, setting, or circumstances in which it occurs, requiring sensitivity to the context.
18. **Communication Gap**: A breakdown in the communication process where the intended message is not understood or received correctly by the other party.

Technical Writing Terminology

1. **Audience Analysis**: The process of understanding the audience's needs, expectations, and level of expertise to tailor technical communication accordingly.
2. **Clarity**: The quality of being easily understood, achieved through concise and straightforward writing without ambiguity.
3. **Conciseness**: The practice of using the fewest words necessary to convey information without losing meaning or clarity.
4. **Precision**: The quality of being exact, accurate, and clear in technical communication, particularly in instructions or specifications.
5. **Abstract**: A brief summary of a research paper, report, or technical document that provides an overview of its main points and findings.
6. **Jargon**: Specialized terms and expressions used by a specific profession or group, which may be unfamiliar to a general audience.
7. **Glossary**: A list of terms and their definitions, typically included in technical documents to help readers understand specialized vocabulary.
8. **Manual**: A detailed document that provides instructions or guidelines on how to perform tasks or operate equipment.
9. **Specification**: A detailed description of the technical requirements, features, and standards that a product or system must meet.
10. **Proposal**: A formal document outlining a plan, project, or solution to a problem, often used in business and technical contexts to request approval or funding.
11. **White Paper**: A detailed, authoritative report or guide that explains a complex issue and presents a solution or recommendation, often used in technical and business environments.

12. **Technical Report**: A document that conveys technical information in a clear, concise, and organized manner, often including research findings, data analysis, and recommendations.
13. **Style Guide**: A set of standards for writing and formatting documents, ensuring consistency in language use, structure, and design across technical documents.
14. **Flowchart**: A diagram that represents a process, system, or algorithm, using shapes and arrows to show steps and their relationships.
15. **Executive Summary**: A brief, comprehensive overview of a larger document or report, designed to give decision-makers the essential points without requiring them to read the entire document.
16. **Usability**: The ease with which a user can navigate and understand a technical document, often assessed through usability testing.
17. **Tone**: The attitude or approach the writer takes towards the audience and subject matter, which in technical writing should be objective, neutral, and professional.
18. **Table of Contents (ToC)**: A list of the sections, chapters, and headings within a document, providing readers with an organized overview of the content.
19. **Index**: An alphabetical list of key terms or topics included at the end of a document, with references to the pages where they appear.
20. **Editing**: The process of reviewing and revising content to improve its clarity, coherence, and correctness before finalizing a technical document

50 Sentences that highlight common writing errors

1. **She *run* every morning.**

   (Error: Incorrect verb form; should be "runs")
2. **Their going to the park later.**

   (Error: Confusion between "their" and "they're")
3. **The teacher gave the students *homeworks* to complete.**

   (Error: Incorrect plural; "homework" is uncountable)
4. **We have less people attending this year.**

   (Error: Use "fewer" instead of "less" for countable nouns)
5. **He didn't *knew* the answer to the question.**

   (Error: Incorrect past tense; should be "know")

6. **The *company's* are growing rapidly.**
   (Error: Misuse of possessive; should be "companies")
7. **She is more *smarter* than him.**
   (Error: Double comparative; should be "smarter")
8. **Everyone *need* to complete their work on time.**
   (Error: Incorrect subject-verb agreement; should be "needs")
9. **I look forward to see you tomorrow.**
   (Error: Missing "to" with infinitive; should be "seeing")
10. **He was tired, *however* he still went for a run.**
    (Error: Improper use of "however"; needs a semicolon or new sentence)
11. **Its a beautiful day outside.**
    (Error: Confusion between "its" and "it's")
12. **The team *was* all excited for the event.**
    (Error: Incorrect subject-verb agreement for plural "team"; should be "were")
13. **Please return the book back when you're done.**
    (Error: Redundant use of "return" and "back")
14. **They didn't *accept* our invitation to the party.**
    (Error: Confusion between "accept" and "except")
15. **The cat chased it's tail.**
    (Error: Incorrect use of possessive; should be "its")
16. **There's many different ways to solve the problem.**
    (Error: "There's" should be "There are" for plural noun "ways")
17. **She does her job very *good.***
    (Error: Incorrect adverb form; should be "well")
18. **The weather has an effect on how *your* feeling today.**
    (Error: Confusion between "your" and "you're")
19. **The *principal* of the matter is trust.**
    (Error: Confusion between "principal" and "principle")
20. **We could of finished the project on time.**
    (Error: Incorrect phrase; should be "could have")

21. **He's the man *who's* car was stolen.**
    (Error: Incorrect possessive; should be "whose")
22. **Me and John are going to the store.**
    (Error: Incorrect pronoun order; should be "John and I")
23. **I can't hardly believe it.**
    (Error: Double negative; should be "can hardly believe")
24. **The book that I read was more better than the movie.**
    (Error: Double comparative; should be "better")
25. **The *amount* of cars on the road has increased.**
    (Error: Use "number" instead of "amount" for countable nouns)
26. **If I was you, I would take the offer.**
    (Error: Incorrect conditional; should be "If I were you")
27. **This is a *compliment* to your skills.**
    (Error: Confusion between "compliment" and "complement")
28. **The kids *done* their homework already.**
    (Error: Incorrect verb form; should be "did")
29. **She will take care of it *irregardless* of the issue.**
    (Error: Incorrect word; should be "regardless")
30. **The house was so big we could of gotten lost.**
    (Error: Incorrect phrase; should be "could have")
31. **I was laying on the couch all day.**
    (Error: Incorrect verb; should be "lying")
32. **He brought me the *principle* results of the study.**
    (Error: Confusion between "principle" and "principal")
33. **Each student must submit their assignments.**
    (Error: Mismatch of singular "each" with plural "their"; can rewrite to "his or her")
34. **We finished the project in less time than we thought.**
    (Error: Should use "fewer" for countable "time units")
35. **There's *to* many mistakes in the report.**
    (Error: Confusion between "to" and "too")
36. **It's a great opportunity for *you're* career.**

(Error: Should be "your" instead of "you're")

37. **The new phone is very *unique*.**

    (Error: "Unique" is an absolute adjective; "very" is unnecessary)

38. **The professor is *real* strict about deadlines.**

    (Error: Incorrect adverb; should be "really")

39. **The group presented *their* final project yesterday.**

    (Error: Should be singular "its" because "group" is collective noun)

40. **He likes football more *then* basketball.**

    (Error: Confusion between "then" and "than")

41. **The data shows that everyone *is* performing better.**

    (Error: "Data" is plural; should be "are")

42. **I have *went* to the gym every day this week.**

    (Error: Incorrect past participle; should be "gone")

43. **She should of called me earlier.**

    (Error: Should be "should have")

44. **This is *one of the best* book I've ever read.**

    (Error: Plural should be used; should be "one of the best books")

45. **My sister *she* is coming to the party.**

    (Error: Redundant pronoun "she"; can delete "she")

46. **The group divided the work between the three of them.**

    (Error: "Between" is used for two; should be "among" for more than two)

47. **The student didn't do *no* work for the assignment.**

    (Error: Double negative; should be "didn't do any work")

48. **It was the more difficult problem of the two.**

    (Error: Should use "more difficult" for comparing two; "most difficult" for more than two)

49. **The team *lead* the project successfully.**

    (Error: Incorrect past tense; should be "led")

50. **She *couldn't hardly* wait to tell him the news.**

    (Error: Double negative; should be "could hardly wait")

17

Seminars and Conferences

Objectives

- To introduce the concept of seminars and conferences.
- To impart knowledge on organizing seminars and conferences.
- To highlight the necessity of such platforms for intellectual and professional exchange.
- To provide insights into the qualities of effective seminars and conferences.

Introduction

Seminars and conferences are platforms for intellectual exchange that have grown significantly in scope and purpose over time. Originally restricted to academic settings, these forums have become indispensable in professional environments. Traditionally, they allowed students and researchers to present their findings through oral or written reports. However, in the modern era, characterized by unprecedented advancements in science and technology, the need for structured intellectual engagement has increased.

These gatherings offer an excellent opportunity for individuals to think collectively, solve complex problems, and plan strategically. They provide the necessary environment for brainstorming and collaboration, ensuring the efficient use of both human and material resources. In this century of rapid technological evolution and global connect ivity, seminars and conferences serve as crucial tools for learning, networking, and driving innovation.

Types of Discussion Groups a) Seminar

A seminar is a focused discussion involving a small group of participants. Typically, a lead speaker presents a detailed paper or research findings, followed by a thorough discussion. The participants, often knowledgeable in the field, interact with the speaker, raising questions, providing insights, and sharing their perspectives.

The primary aim of a seminar is to promote knowledge exchange and generate new ideas. These discussions can foster innovation and deepen participants' understanding of a subject, making seminars an invaluable tool for both academic and professional development.

b) Symposium

In a symposium, multiple experts discuss various aspects of a central topic, often for the benefit of a broader audience. Each speaker is allotted a specific time to present their views. While formal in structure, symposia encourage audience interaction, making them dynamic and engaging.

These events are suitable for large gatherings, where diverse viewpoints can be explored systematically. By incorporating audience questions, symposia also introduce an element of spontaneity that enhances understanding and engagement.

c) Panel Discussion

A panel discussion brings together experts to deliberate on a specific question or issue. Unlike symposia, where speakers deliver separate speeches, panel members interact directly, creating a cooperative dialogue.

Audience participation often follows, allowing listeners to pose questions and contribute to the discussion. This format is particularly effective in public forums, such as radio and television programs, where diverse perspectives on pressing issues can be explored.

d) Conference

Conferences are more extensive gatherings compared to seminars and symposia. They bring together individuals with shared interests to discuss a central theme or subject. These events often include lectures, audiovisual presentations, and exhibitions.

Conferences typically feature multiple sessions running simultaneously, allowing participants to choose topics of interest. Registration is usually required, making these events exclusive and focused. Conferences often conclude with actionable recommendations, making them highly impactful for organizations and industries.

e) Colloquium

A colloquium is an organized event where scholars or experts discuss a specific subject. These gatherings are intellectually stimulating and provide deep insights into niche areas of study.

f) Convention

Conventions are structured meetings designed for professionals, associations, or political groups. They focus on matters of shared interest, emphasizing fellowship and networking. These gatherings often result in significant resolutions and strategies relevant to the group's objectives.

Key Elements of Oral Communication

Effective communication is the cornerstone of successful seminars and conferences. The six key elements are:

1. **Pitch:** Pitch refers to the tone of voice, influenced by the vibration of vocal cords. A varied pitch keeps the audience engaged and conveys emotions effectively.
2. **Volume:** Volume is crucial for ensuring that the speaker's message reaches all attendees. A balanced volume, neither too loud nor too soft, is essential for maintaining interest.
3. **Rate:** The rate of speech determines its clarity. Speaking too fast may confuse the audience, while a slow pace may lose their attention.
4. **Quality:** The tone and clarity of the voice contribute to its quality. A pleasant and well-modulated voice enhances the listener's experience.
5. **Animation:** The liveliness of a speaker's delivery, or animation, keeps the audience engaged.

6. **Pause:** Strategic pauses emphasize key points and allow the audience to absorb information.

The Role of Personal Appearance

A speaker's personal appearance significantly impacts their credibility and rapport with the audience.

Posture

Good posture conveys confidence and professionalism. Standing tall and maintaining an open stance encourages trust and engagement.

Eye Contact

Eye contact is vital for connecting with the audience. It fosters trust and ensures effective interaction. A speaker should engage with all sections of the audience, avoiding distractions like looking at the floor or ceiling.

Voice

A strong and clear voice enhances delivery. Speakers can improve their voice through practice, such as reading aloud and listening to recordings for self-evaluation.

Engaging the Audience

Understanding the audience is crucial for a successful presentation. Factors like age, background, and interests should influence the speaker's approach. Adding humor, personal anecdotes, or dramatizing ideas can captivate listeners and foster a connection.

Preparation

Preparation is essential for any successful seminar or conference. While a written script may be used for complex presentations, familiarity with the material is crucial for maintaining natural interaction. Notes on cards can help speakers stay on track without reading verbatim.

Visual Aids

Visual aids like slides, charts, and videos enhance the effectiveness of a presentation. However, they should be used sparingly to support key points without overwhelming the audience.

Organizing Seminars and Conferences

Organizing a seminar or conference requires meticulous planning:

- **Define Objectives**: Clearly outline the purpose of the event.
- **Select Speakers and Participants**: Choose knowledgeable individuals to lead discussions.
- **Plan Logistics**: Arrange a suitable venue and schedule.
- **Communicate Details**: Share information about the event with participants well in advance.
- **Coordinate Sessions**: Ensure smooth transitions and address logistical needs.

Questions

1. What are the key elements of oral communication? Explain how each element contributes to an effective spoken presentation.
2. Differentiate between a seminar, symposium, and panel discussion. What are the specific communication skills required for each format?
3. Discuss the importance of audience awareness and feedback in oral communication during a seminar or symposium.
4. How does the role of a moderator differ in a panel discussion compared to a symposium? What communication skills are essential for this role?
5. What are the common barriers to effective oral communication in group settings like panel discussions and how can they be overcome?
6. Explain the role of body language, voice modulation, and eye contact in enhancing the effectiveness of oral presentations. Provide examples from seminar experiences.

Index